On the Trail of the Catahoula

On the Trail of the Catahoula: A Geographical Investigation

ISBN: 978-1-60801-202-2

Cover and book design by Alex Dimeff.

Cover photograph: "Catahoula Leopard Dog" by Krystal Hamlin, https://flic.kr/p/yBhzvh.

Printed in the United States of America on acid-free paper.

UNIVERSITY OF NEW ORLEANS PRESS
2000 Lakeshore Drive
New Orleans, Louisiana 70148
unopress.org

On the Trail of the Catahoula

A Geographical Investigation

by Walter LeBon

UNIVERSITY OF NEW ORLEANS PRESS

This work is dedicated to
Milton Newton,
a good friend and a great geographer.

CONTENTS

FOREWORD

I started research on the Catahoula cur as a grad student in geography at Louisiana State University in the 1960s. The Catahoula, and his part in the cultural and physical landscapes was the topic of my master's thesis, *The Catahoula Hog Dog—A Cultural Trait of the Upland South,* which is in LSU's Middleton Library today. In 2008, I wrote a monograph, *The Louisiana Catahoula Leopard: A Geographical Investigation.* It was published by Geoscience Publications.

In the 1960s, when I started my research, little factual material was known about the Catahoula, although there was a lot of folklore about him. If the internet existed, it wasn't used for scholarly research.

Chapters 1 through 4 appear largely as written, in the sixties, based on fieldwork and a search of printed material done at the time. In the field, I discovered that the Catahoula was a "cur" and what that meant to the people who used it. In the course of my fieldwork, I learned what a cur was, and in time I learned that this type of dog contributed mightily to the survival of early colonial settlements and with the success of the frontier in settling America.

Besides the Catahoula, there are a number of other cur breeds in the southern U.S. In the sixties, many of the people who knew about one cur breed didn't know about the others. Now, thanks largely to the internet, where many cur breeds have their own web sites, there is more widespread knowledge of cur breeds. Later chapters of this work draw upon present-day knowledge and research I've done since my last publication, in 2008.

Walter LeBon
Mirabilis Gardens
April, 2021

INTRODUCTION

For as long as anyone remembers, a strangely spotted, white-eyed dog has been chasing hogs around northern Louisiana. People generally call him the Catahoula, the Catahoula hog dog, or the Catahoula cur. Since 1979, he has been Louisiana's state dog, and our state government calls him the Louisiana Catahoula leopard dog. Many Louisianians don't know the dog exists, but those who do believe the breed originated in Louisiana. In fact, both an area lake and a parish are named Catahoula. Folklore insists the Catahoula descended from Spanish war dogs brought to Louisiana in 1541-42 by Hernando De Soto. The war dogs, mastiffs, supposedly bred with Native Americans' dogs and wolves. The red wolf was the wolf native to the southern United States.

Three of the Catahoula's characteristics have made him an object of keen interest both to people interested in dogs, and to students of Louisiana lore. First, there's his unusual appearance. Catahoulas are smooth-haired dogs, and come in many colors, but the most prized is the leopard. Figures In-1 and In-2 illustrate the leopard trait. Leopards have irregular dark splotches. Leopards have a genetic condition called "merling" although most Catahoula people don't use that term. These splotches may be black on a gray background as in Figure In-1 (these are "blue" leopards), or reddish brown on a lighter reddish background as in Figure In-2 (red leopards). Most leopards have one or two "glass" eyes. The dog in Figure In-2 has two glass eyes. Notice the white irises. In Figure In-3, is a dog with one glass eye and one "cracked" eye. The iris in the dog's left eye is white with a brown "crack."

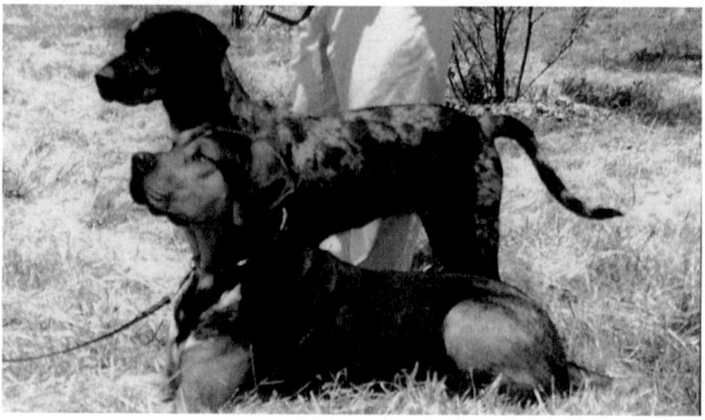

Above: Fig. In-1 The dog in back is a blue leopard. The dog in front is merled (not as obviously) but also has genes for black-and-tan coloration.

Below: Fig. In-2 A beautiful glass-eyed red leopard. Both images courtesy of Vicki Loudenslager.

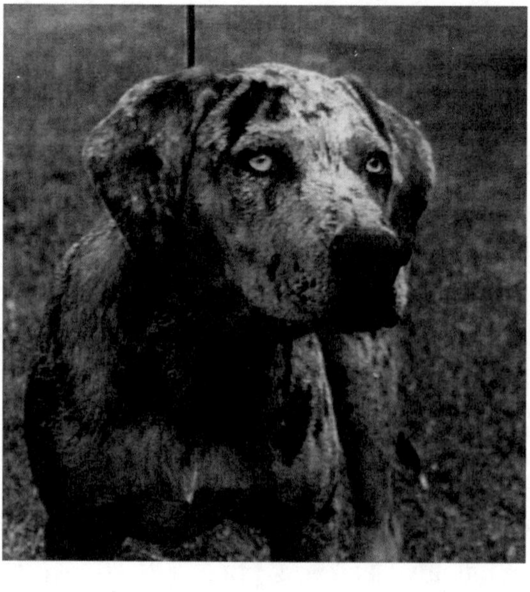

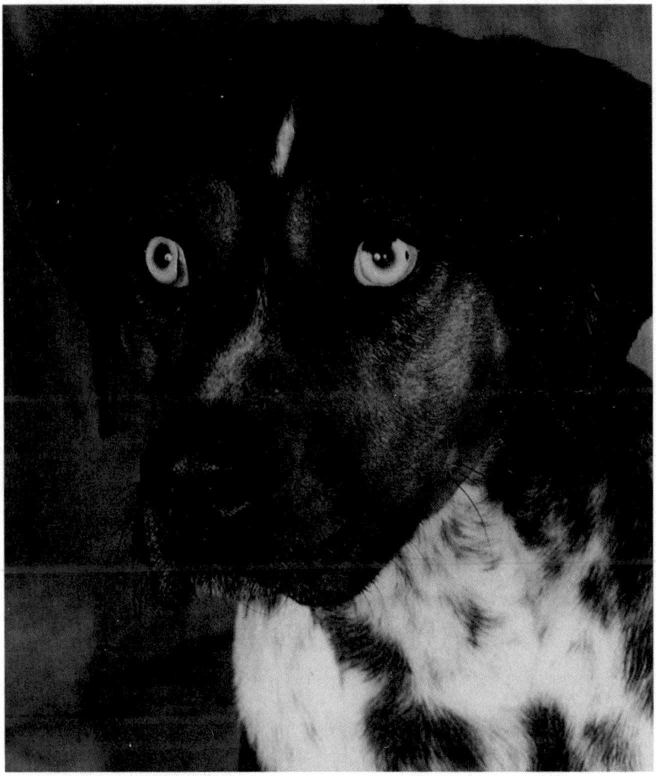

Fig. In-3 A Catahoula with one glass eye and one “cracked” eye. Notice the brown crack in his left eye. Image courtesy of Vicki Loudenslager.

The second unusual characteristic of Catahoulas involves their ability to do something very few other dogs can do. Catahoulas can go into a swampy woodland with a hog hunter, catch a wild boar, and hold him (that's right "hold" a wild boar) until the hunter catches up. The dogs (often two) position themselves on opposite sides of a boar's head and grab an ear or jowl (Figures 3.3c and 3.3d). If the boar turns to attack one dog, the other will yank his ear, and the hog will turn to confront that dog. In this way, the exasperated boar can be kept from running while the hunter is fighting his way through underbrush to the scene of the action.

The third characteristic is the ability of Catahoulas to gather wild hogs in a pen. Other kinds of dogs, and some Catahoulas, have been killed trying to do this. Wild boars are not like sheep who tend to run from dogs, but grown wild boars, with their sows and pigs, refuse to be driven by dogs who weigh less than a quarter of their own weight. In the nineteenth and early twentieth centuries, hog raisers, or those who claimed ownership of the feral hogs in Louisiana's forests and swamps, built pens along the rivers and bayous that thread the area. Two wings, disguised with brush, served to funnel the hogs into the pen. On finding a herd of wild hogs, a Catahoula will attack the boar, until the infuriated boar, followed by his whole herd, chases the dog toward the pen. If the boar loses interest, the dog will go back and attack him again. In this way, the dog will eventually get the hogs in the pen, and the dog will jump the fence while his owner closes the gate. During the steamboat era hog pens were built on stream banks, where hogs could be loaded onto the boats.

I am a native of New Orleans, not a part of the state where Catahoulas are used. A cousin, who lived north of

Lake Pontchartrain, had a blue leopard named "Lassie" (a misnomer if there ever was one.) Animals, especially unusual breeds of domesticated animals, have always interested me. Twenty years later, I was in graduate school at LSU and working on an MA in geography. When my major professor, Dr. Milton Newton suggested I write my thesis on the Catahoula, I jumped at the chance.

My thesis was to be evaluated, and I was to be questioned, by a committee made up of three professors. One of them was Dr. Fred B. Kniffen, one of the foremost geographers in the United States and a revered professor at LSU. Some theses, on being read by Dr. Kniffen, had elicited the response: "But is it geography?" These words had deflated the ego of many an LSU geography student. I wasn't sure what my answer would be, but I was determined to think long and hard about it and do my best.

I searched the library at LSU and the East Baton Rouge Parish Library. I drove up to the Catahoula Parish Library in Harrisonburg, the parish seat. I searched not only for "Catahoula," but for anything I could find on stock dogs. I talked with dog fanciers, animal husbandry teachers, farmers, and people who owned Catahoulas. I went on hog hunts and observed Catahoulas first hand. I studied canine genetics and traced the history of dogs in the southern United States.

This book is the result of my investigation: the story of the Louisiana Catahoula.

CHAPTER ONE
WHERE DO I START?

In 1964, I graduated from LSUNO (now the University of New Orleans). I taught high school for a couple of years before enrolling in graduate school at LSU. I was studying geography, my favorite subject since grade school. Geography is defined a number of ways, but academically, at LSU, geography was "the study of the earth as the home of humans." Geographers ask questions like: How do the people in this area get a living from their environment? How does their culture relate to their environment? Geography is not just the study of the earth (that's geology), but of the relationship between people and their environment—and animals are part of that environment.

I was searching for a topic for my master's thesis when my advisor, Dr. Milton Newton, suggested I write on the Catahoula hog dog, aka the Catahoula cur. The Catahoula is famous (at least locally) as a breed developed in Louisiana. I would have to search for the origin of the breed and its place in the lives of the people.

The place of origin wasn't in dispute. Everyone believed the Catahoula originated in Louisiana, but from what kinds of dog was it developed? Could the dogs of the Native Americans corral feral hogs as Catahoulas can? Did early European settlers bring dogs that would develop into Catahoulas?

I've always been interested in animals, especially domesticated animals, so when Dr. Newton suggested I research the Catahoula, I jumped at the chance. Geographical research is like detective work. The first step is gathering clues. How much is already known about this topic? Has anyone researched it before? Geographers start this kind of research in the library, at least they did in the 1960s, when I wrote my thesis. In my library research, I discovered many newspaper articles and a few magazine articles about the Catahoula. Almost every article said exactly the same things; it was as if the authors were simply paraphrasing one another. Some described the dog and its abilities without discussing its origin. Those who speculated on the Catahoula's origin credited the Spanish explorer Hernando De Soto with bringing some of the Catahoula's ancestors to Louisiana—a theory commonly held in the sixties and still held by many Louisianans today.

The only exception to this trend was an article in a 1950 issue of *Farm Quarterly* written by Sam Mims of Minden, LA. Mims described the Catahoula and talked about its utility, but what made his article unique was his statement that some thought the Catahoula related to "a spotted dog from the Rhine Valley."[1] Mr. Mims gave no sources and didn't indicate who thought the Catahoula was related to the Rhine Valley dog. I wrote to Mr. Mims, but Mrs. Mims replied that her husband had gone blind and wouldn't be able to help me. Having come to a dead end, I decided to check out the De Soto theory.

In 1539, De Soto and his party of almost a thousand Spaniards landed in the area Ponce de Leon had named "La Florida" some twenty-five years before. Searching for a rich empire they believed existed in the American hinterland, the Spaniards explored the southeast of what is now the United States. In 1541, De Soto reached the Mississippi River where, today, it separates Mississippi from Arkansas.

1 Sam Mims. "Hog Dogs" *Farm Quarterly Vol. 5, No. 1,* 1950 P. 77.

The Spaniards crossed the great river, traversed Arkansas, explored parts of Oklahoma and Texas, then, probably doubting the existence of any rich empire north of Mexico, turned back. Upon again reaching the Mississippi, assuming the great southward-flowing river emptied into the Gulf of Mexico, the party traveled downriver, intending to reach Mexico. De Soto died of a fever, possibly in Louisiana. His men sank his weighted body in the river to keep their leader's death secret from the Native Americans. His expedition, by then greatly diminished, did eventually reach Spanish settlements in Mexico. In 1542, then, De Soto's party skirted what was to become the home of the Catahoula leopard dog. De Soto may be there still.

Two of the stories about the origin of the Catahoula link De Soto's expedition and the indigenous people of eastern Louisiana. Most of the articles I had found hold that the Catahoula descended from Spanish war dogs left by De Soto, probably with admixtures of native American dogs and red wolves, a species native to the southeastern U.S. The Louisiana Tourist Development Commission propagates this legend in a pamphlet:

> Hog dogs, thought by some to be a cross between dogs owned by Indians and Dalmatians (which crossed the Bering Strait) … were recorded as 'being present' when De Soto landed in Jonesville, Louisiana in 1542.[2]

Interesting story, but early explorers in Louisiana wrote about the dogs of the native people they encountered, and

2 Louisiana Tourist Development Commission. The Catahoula Hog Dog Was Hunting Here When Spanish Conquistadores First Stomped into the South. (Baton Rouge: Louisiana Tourist Development Commission, 1966)

none of their reports mention anything about dogs resembling either Dalmatians or Catahoulas.

The other legend insists that the Spanish *brought* the Catahoula to Louisiana, rather than simply recording its presence. W. C. Brown, in an anthology he compiled, advances this theory:

> It is claimed by some, after years of research, that this strain of dog originated in Spain where, in feudal times, they guarded the entrances to castles and fortresses … the Spanish explorers used them both as guards and scouts. By following this theory, one is almost certain to conclude that the Indians who lived in or near the mound city of Aniloo (now Jonesville) captured some of these dogs from De Soto's stalwarts when he visited there.[3]

Unsure which tribe would have captured some of the Spanish war dogs, Brown describes another theory: that it was the Natchez, from east of the Mississippi River:

> They, the Natchez Indians, would cross the Mississippi River into what is now Concordia and Catahoula Parishes and make raids on the Choctaw Indians who were natives of this area. It is said that the Natchez Indians used their vicious dogs to drive the Choctaws from their villages so they could loot them.[4]

What evidence is there that De Soto's party had Catahoula-like dogs in the first place? Researching the Span-

3 W. C. Brown (editor). "Introduction" The Catahoula Hog Dog. (Harrisonburg, LA: privately printed. 1962)
4 Ibid.

ish conquistadores and explorers, I learned that they, De Soto included, did indeed use war dogs. Native Americans were apparently terrified of these mastiff-like dogs. Miguel León-Portilla wrote of Spanish-Indian conflicts in his book *The Broken Spears.*[5] In this work, León-Portilla quotes an Aztec scribe:

> Their eyes are enormous, with flat ears and long dangling tongues. The color of their eyes is a burning yellow, their eyes flash and shoot off sparks. Their bellies are hollow, their flanks long and narrow. They bound here and there, panting, with their tongues hanging out. And they are spotted like an ocelot.

"Spotted like an ocelot!" Sounds like a Catahoula leopard! Could these dogs have been here in present-day Louisiana since De Soto's time? If so, they must have been seen by the first Europeans to come into the area after DeSoto.

In fact, many writers state that Henri de Tonti, or Tonti the Iron Hand, saw Catahoula-like dogs on a 1686 visit to the Natchitoches Indians. Tonti had been a companion of René-Robert Cavalier, Sieur de la Salle in 1682, when La Salle claimed this land he named Louisiana for France. Tonti had earned his "Iron Hand" appellation when he lost a hand in a European war and had it replaced with some iron device. In 1686, Tonti explored the Red River and visited the Natchitoches. John Blanchard tells of Tonti's trip up the Red River in an article in *Forests and People*[6]:

---

5 Miguel Leon-Portilla (ed.) The Broken Spears. (Boston: Beacon Press.-1962)

6 John Blanchard. "Hog Dogs of the Catahoula" Forests and People Vol. 11 No.1. 1961.

> In 1682 [1686] five [four] years after he descended the Mississippi with LaSalle, Tonti the Iron Hand trekked cross-country to visit the Natchitoches Indians, being accompanied by scouts from the Taensas tribe. In brief notes he told of seeing a number of dogs with white eyes and mottled spots.

Older geographical and historical texts refer to the first Europeans to traverse parts of North America as "early travelers." I was frankly surprised to find a number of primary records of these early travelers, including a memoir written by none other than Tonti, at the Middleton Library at LSU. Despite Blanchard's claim, a search of Tonti's memoir[7] reveals no mention of such "dogs with white eyes and mottled spots." Tonti's account of his ill-fated trip mentions only four dogs, all of which he ate to keep from starving. He was apparently too hungry to bother describing any of the dogs; he mentions only that two were his and two belonged to Native Americans.

Most early travelers in Louisiana do not mention dogs at all. Certainly, there were dogs present, but people do not mention the commonplace. Catahoulas, with their unusual eyes and coloration, would have been mentioned.

Two early travelers, Antoine-Simon Le Page du Pratz and Father Pierre de Charlevoix, did describe Native American dogs. Du Pratz spent the years 1718 through 1734 in Louisiana, where he befriended people of the Natchez tribe and learned their language. In a history published in Paris[8], Le Page du Pratz compares the red wolf, native to Louisiana, to a European wolf:

---

7 Henri de Tonti. "Memoir" in French B. F. (ed.) Historical Collections of Louisiana. (New York: Wiley and Putnam 1846)

8 Antoine S. Le Page du Pratz. The history of Louisiana or of the Western Parts of Virginia and Carolina. (Paris: De Bure 1758)

> He is not so brown as our wolves, nor so fierce and dangerous; he is therefore more like a dog than a wolf, especially the dogs of the natives, who differs from him in nothing, but that he [the Native American's dog] barks.

According to du Pratz, then, the Native Americans' dogs looked like wolves, not like Catahoulas. Likewise, Father Pierre de Charlevoix, traversing the area in 1721 and 1722, reported that although some of the Louisiana dogs were black and white, "they appear to be all of one species, with upright ears and a long snout, like that of a wolf."[9] Catahoulas do not have upright ears.

Alfred Kroeber, one of the foremost anthropologists of the first half of the twentieth century, studied dogs of many North American indigenous peoples. Kroeber interviewed elderly American Indians, studied pictographs, and found mummified dogs. Kroeber reported variations in size, hair length, and color, but found that dogs of almost all tribes had "prick" ears, like wolves.[10] Charlevoix called them "upright" ears (or the French equivalent thereof). Whichever name you choose to use, they stand above a dog's head. Catahoulas have pendant ears, which hang down alongside their heads.

In summary, I found no evidence that Catahoulas, or their ancestors, were either left in present-day Louisiana by De Soto's sixteenth-century expedition or that their presence predated De Soto's arrival. Nor did I find evidence of Catahoula-like dogs in Louisiana in the seventeenth or eighteenth centuries. Don Abney, a writer and breeder of Cata-

9 Pierre F. X. de Charlevoix. "Historical Journal of Father Pierre Francois Xavier de Charlevoix" in French, B. F. Historical Collections of Louisiana. (New York: D. Appleton and Company. 1851)

10 Alfred L. Kroeber. "Culture Element Distribution XV: Salt, Dogs, and Tobacco" Berkeley Anthropological Records 21(1). 1941.21(1),1941.

houlas, relates a statement made by Mrs. George Traxler of Lake Providence, LA, in the 1930s. Mrs. Traxler who was of Native American and French ancestry, contended that "the dogs [Catahoulas] came with the white man from the east."[11] Clues I discovered later lead me to agree with Mrs. Traxler.

One frequently heard story holds that Jim Bowie and his brother Rezin owned Catahoulas, and each was protected by a Catahoula at the foot of his bed every night. The Bowie family came to Louisiana from Kentucky in 1802. Jim was six years old. The Bowie family settled on Bushley Bayou, in what was then Rapides Parish, not far from Catahoula Lake. In 1814, Jim enlisted in the Louisiana militia to fight in the Battle of New Orleans but arrived too late for the battle. Jim lived in several places in Louisiana and was often in trouble over land sales, or in league with his friend, Jean Lafitte, smuggling. Bowie left Louisiana for Texas around 1830 and met death at the Alamo in 1836.

Jim Bowie was a renowned fighter. Even so, the statement his mother made, when told of his death, surprised me. Jim's mother said of her courageous son: "I'll wager no wounds were found in his back."[12]

I've found no definite record of Jim or Rezin Bowie owning Catahoulas, but, as we'll see later, there is reason to believe that Catahoulas came to Louisiana with the same wave of settlers as the Bowies.

After a thorough search of library sources, I called the LSU College of Agriculture and asked for information

---

11 Don Abney. The Louisiana Catahoula Leopard Dog. (Wilsonville, OR: Doral Publishing Company 1996.)

12 Tom Faranda. "What Jim Bowie's Mother Said" Tom Faranda's Folly. Last modified Jan. 3, 2009. Tomfaranda.typad.com/folly/2009/01/what-jim-bowie's-mother-said-after-she-was-told-of-his-death…

on the Catahoula. The lady who answered said she'd ask around and promised to get back to me. The next day a professor called and said the Catahoula wasn't used in modern stock raising and that no one at the college knew much about it. He added that he had, on a number of occasions seen feral hogs resting on the side of the highway near Turkey Creek, LA.

Whenever the dog came to Louisiana, its name certainly suggests the breed originated around Catahoula Lake or in Catahoula Parish. Catahoula Lake was in Catahoula Parish until the legislature, in all its wisdom, divided the parish and named the half with the lake LaSalle Parish. The other half is Catahoula Parish.

Both the lake and the parish are in the Mississippi River's flood plain. With my archival research at a stopping point, this seemed like a good place to see some Catahoulas in action.

CHAPTER TWO
IN THE FIELD

The many articles I had read described Catahoulas, both those that had the distinctive leopard markings and those that didn't, and told of their extraordinary abilities, but the accounts of the breed's origin were pure conjecture. I had known from the beginning that I'd not likely solve the mystery of the Catahoula's origin in the library. In rural areas, especially in the South, a lot of knowledge of the kind I was seeking is passed from generation to generation and never gets into libraries.

I looked forward to working in "the field," which is what geographers call the actual place and/or culture they're studying. Some of the Catahoula behaviors I'd read about were hard to imagine. I'd read descriptions of their unsurpassed ability to herd cattle and hunt hogs; now I wanted to see them in action. I had to learn as much as I could about their physical and behavioral characteristics. I wanted to talk with people who knew them. Maybe no one could tell me the origin of the dog, but if I could learn what the Catahoula was like, I could search for similar breeds and perhaps get a clue to the Catahoula's origin that way.

I was planning my drive up to Catahoula Parish when, at lunch one spring day in 1969, I spotted Ian Gravel in the LSU cafeteria. Ian was a classmate from a geology course we had taken the previous semester. Ian was about six feet tall and muscular. He was a geology major, and he had told me about his older brother, Johnny, a geologist for a major oil company.

Over lunch, I told Ian about my research on the Catahoula, and he surprised me by inviting me on a hog hunt scheduled for the very next day. It turned out that Johnny was coming to pick Ian up in the morning. Johnny had two Catahoulas that he kept at their parents' home in LaSalle Parish. I agreed to meet them in the Student Union parking lot.

We met next morning at 5:30. Johnny, a light-haired version of Ian, had graduated two years prior. On the way to their parents' home, the three of us talked about Catahoulas and dogs in general. I was surprised when Johnny claimed he had seen Collies with the same coat condition that Catahoula leopards have, glass eyes and all, a condition known as "merling." Ian mentioned that deer hunters were always glad to have hogs removed from the forest because they compete with deer for food. Not only acorns, Ian said, but berries and some kinds of foliage.

In an hour or so we were at my friends' parents' home on a dirt road west of Catahoula Lake. The house was less than half a mile off the highway, and surrounded by hardwood forest. There was more sunlight in the forest than there would be in midsummer, and since it was early spring, not all of the trees had their full complement of leaves. I love being in a forest. I enjoy looking for trees that are unusual or new to me. If I had grown up in a rural area, I probably would have been a forester. This was a bottomland hardwood forest, the kind that thrives in the flood plain of the Mississippi and other Southern rivers.

The Gravel boys introduced me to their parents, and we visited over a cup of good coffee. When we finished, the boys got their rifles, each a Winchester, and we went out back of the house. There, in a kennel with chain-link fencing, were two female Catahoulas. Each was a little over knee high and smooth haired with pendant, triangular ears and tails shaped like inverted question marks. One was Julie, a five-year-old with glass eyes. Her kennel-mate, April, a year or two younger, was black except for one white foot and a small white area on her chest. I knew Julie was a Catahoula because of her coloring, but if I hadn't been told she was Catahoula, I wouldn't have known it. Asked how you could tell a Catahoula from their appearance, Johnny said the only real way was by their behavior when hunting.

Johnny told me about two brindled Catahoulas their dad had owned. Brindled animals are light tan to dark brown and have black vertical stripes (Fig. 2.1). Occasionally a brindle has so much black, he appears to be black with brown stripes. Ian said there was a breed called the treeing Tennessee brindle. About ten years ago, he said, a preacher had gathered brindled Catahoulas and similar dogs to create the treeing Tennessee brindle.

We entered the woods and followed the dogs, attempting to keep close enough to them to be on hand when they caught a hog. The dogs stayed with one another, but instead of sniffing the ground, as I had expected, they hunted with their heads up. Hounds, Johnny said, hunted with their noses to the ground, but Catahoulas weren't hounds. Once we lost track of the dogs and stood around catching our breath. I hoped the dogs weren't lost, but my companions didn't seem concerned. After a few minutes, we heard a lot of barking off to our right. We started running in that direction, but just as I was going around a huge palmetto, Johnny yelled "Walt, stop!" On the ground, ahead of me, was something as white as a cotton boll.

In the second it took me to realize it was the wide-open mouth of a water moccasin, Johnny put a bullet into the gaping white mouth, and the snake collapsed.

When my legs stopped shaking, we continued toward the barking, and Ian yelled, "The dogs have something cornered in the baygall (a small swampy area) by the old road." We entered the baygall, and came on the dogs. They were on either side of a squealing sow, struggling to hold onto her ears. I was elated to see something I had read about happening before my eyes. The sow was bigger than either of the dogs and was desperately trying to break free. This quote, from a historian of the frontier, illustrates the tenaciousness of a cur holding an animal:

> [In the 1880s] … a cavalry troop had adopted a cur as a mascot. The troopers enjoyed telling a story about their dog and a buffalo. The cur had chased and caught a buffalo, grabbed his jaw, and refused to let go. The buffalo, after a lot of ineffective shaking, sped off with the dog hanging from his jaw. The troopers had to kill the buffalo to get their dog back! The cur is definitely a hold dog![13]

Ian dispatched the sow with a bullet to the head, an excellent shot considering the proximity to the dogs' heads. Satisfied with their kill, the brothers judged that the sow would provide some good meals for their parents.

Years after I completed my thesis, I found this quote from one Leak Bevil, a native of the Big Thicket area of east Texas:

---

13 John Baur. Dogs on the Frontier. The Naylor Company. San Antonio. 1964.

> You can take a good dog and round up a bunch of hogs and he'll hold 'em right there, and you can sit on your horse and just ... rope a young one and pull him up on the saddle and mark 'im. He'd catch 'im by the ear. I'm speakin' of pigs now, pigs we never marked, not hogs.[14]

Ian and Johnny hung the sow by the back legs from a branch of a live oak. I had never seen an animal field dressed, and the mass of organs they pulled out of the sow amazed me. Julie relaxed and caught her breath while April poked through the offal, looking for something to eat. The offal must have amounted to half the animal's weight. Ian tied a large black garbage bag to his back, and Johnny and I hoisted the hog and tied it onto his shoulders. Forty-five minutes later, we were back at the house.

I had now seen Catahoulas in action. I had noticed three things that might help me find other breeds to which they may be related. First: They had hunted with their heads up, rather than sniffing along the ground. This, Johnny had said, meant they weren't hounds. (I later learned that scent hounds sniff the ground to find their quarry. There is another type of hound, sight hounds, which hunt with their heads up. When Southern hunters use the word "hound," they usually mean scent hound.) Second: They had not barked while searching for their quarry. Third: They'd had a unique way of keeping the sow from running. Just as I had read, each of Johnny's Catahoulas had taken a grip on an ear. Neither Ian, Johnny, nor their dad knew much about the origin of the Catahoula. They had heard the De Soto story, but didn't know whether it were true.

---

14 Campbell and Lynn Loughmiller. *The Big Thicket Legacy.* University of Texas Press. Austin. 1977.

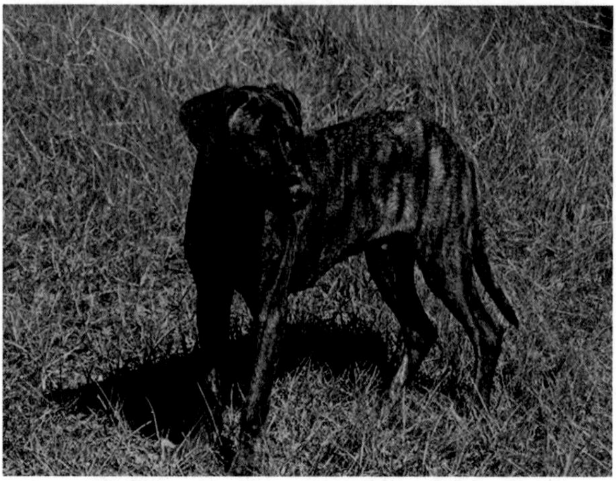

Fig. 2.1 Brindle Catahoulas, once fairly common, are now less so. Image courtesy of Tori Earls.

After the hunt, impressed by my first experience with Catahoulas in action, I decided to pursue my original plan and drive through the flood plain from west of Baton Rouge toward Catahoula Parish, with people about their dogs along the way. I was sure there were Catahoula leopards in every parish in Louisiana, and many other places as well, but I started my field work in the Mississippi's flood plain because there, there was a parish and a lake both named Catahoula. The dog must have some connection there.

On an unusually warm day in the spring of 1969, I crossed the Mississippi and drove west of Baton Rouge. After I passed the restaurants and gas stations, I turned north, into flat country dotted with sugar cane fields; this was the flood plain of the Mississippi River. Before the levees were built, in spring, when the river was high, the flood plain was often under water. Higher places on the flood plain, one or two feet higher, were mostly natural levees of former channels of the Mississippi or one of its tributaries. These "ridges" had been left behind as the river snaked its way across the flood plain.

I spoke with many people who owned or had owned the dogs, some who used them to round up cattle, some who hunted hogs with Catahoulas, and many who kept them as watch dogs or pets. One lady I spoke with emphasized her Catahoula's protectiveness. Her young children sometimes played in a place she couldn't see well from her house, but she said, "As long as that dog's with my kids, I don't worry about 'em."

Twice I was offered puppies, but as I had two dogs at home, I declined. Many people told me how smart their dogs were. When I taught high school in New Orleans, before beginning my graduate program, I'd noticed that when kids talked about their dogs, their dogs were always exceptionally intelligent. It seems the same is true of adults.

As I drove northward, I didn't stick to the main roads. I figured people in less populated places were less busy and more likely to talk. I stopped at many rural grocery stores and gas stations and inquired about Catahoulas. I asked whether they were still used locally, and for the names of people who might be able to tell me about them. I saw a number of Catahoulas along the way.

If a dog wasn't merled, I couldn't be sure it was a Catahoula. Most breeds of dogs have distinctive appearances. Even people who don't pay much attention to dogs can tell at a glance whether a dog is a collie, poodle, or Boston terrier—but individual Catahoulas, perhaps because they're valued for their abilities rather than adherence to some aesthetic standard, tend to look like mutts, varying widely in size and color. The exception is the Catahoula leopard, with its trademark dark splotches on a lighter background.

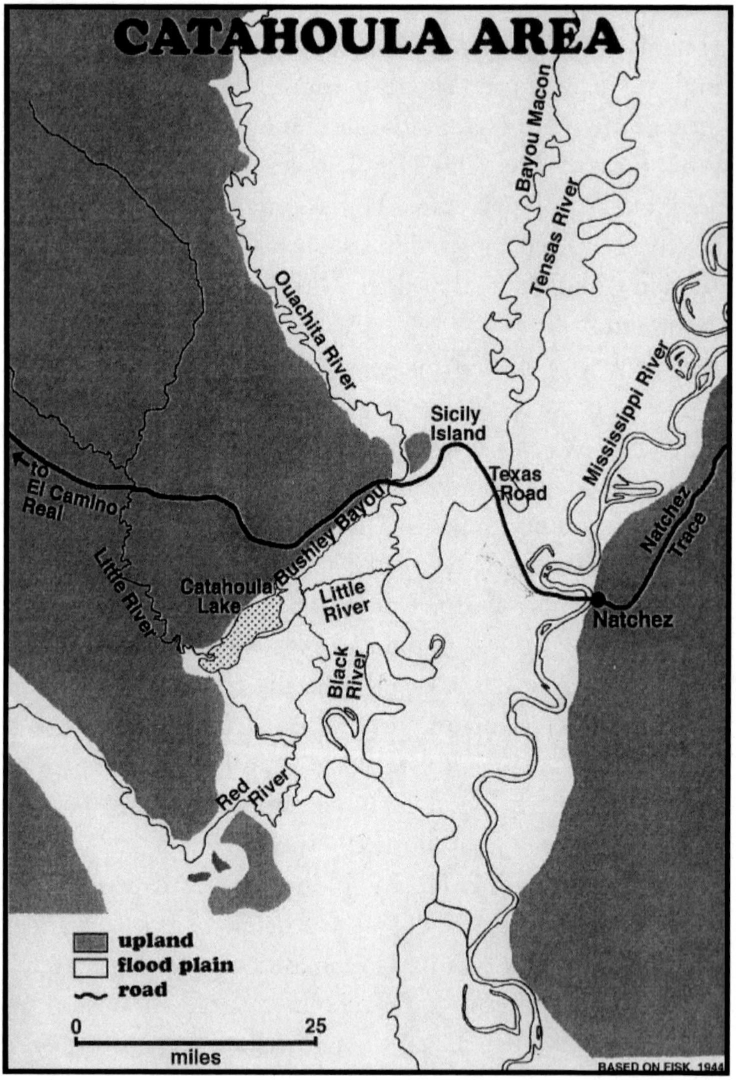
CATAHOULA AREA
Bayou Macon
Tensas River
Ouachita River
Mississippi River
Sicily Island
Texas Road
to El Camino Real
Bushley Bayou
Natchez Trace
Natchez
Little River
Catahoula Lake
Little River
Black River
Red River
upland
flood plain
road
0
25
miles
BASED ON FISK, 1944

Map 1.1

I think my advisor, Dr. Milton Newton, came up with the answer. Until the mid-twentieth century, there was no organization for registering Catahoulas. A farmer or hog hunter getting a Catahoula pup couldn't ask for the dog's registration papers—but, if the dog was a leopard, the buyer knew the dog likely had Catahoula blood. The leopard condition is a form of folk registration even today.

Early in the afternoon of my first day in the field, I was passing a weather-beaten grocery store when I noticed a dog I thought was a Catahoula. The dog was sleeping beside a thin young man on the tail gate of a blue Ford pickup. On closer inspection, the dog was definitely unusual. He was colored like a Catahoula leopard but had the build and ears of a basset hound.

When I got out of my car and started to ask about the dog, the young man raised his hand and motioned that I should wait. "Watch that crow yonder flyin' toward that sycamore."

Across the road was a small sycamore tree. As the crow reached it, a smaller bird burst from the foliage and flew straight at the crow. The crow fled with the smaller bird on his tail.

"It's a mocker," the young man said. "Every spring, when they're nestin' they get ornery and won't let no crows near their nest."

"It is surprising to see that little bird chasing the much bigger crow," I replied, "but what kind of dog do you have there?" I motioned toward the dog, who had lifted his head, glared at me, then gone back to sleep.

"Ah really don't know nuthin' bout this dawg," the young man said. "Name's Bougaloo, but ah only had 'im fer two days. Feller give 'im to me when he took a job in Houston. You're lucky that sumbitch ain't here. He'd bend yer ear fer a hour. Sumbitch talks too much. He could talk a starvin' dog off a meat truck." I hadn't learned anything from my first "interview," but it was amusing.

I enjoyed my first day in the field, but I hadn't gained much information. I wondered whether the whole thing was a waste of time.

A week or so later, I had another chance to drive up to the Catahoula country. I drove further north and noticed a post office vehicle parked under a beautiful red maple. When I saw a mailman walking toward the vehicle, I asked whether he knew of someone I could talk with about Catahoulas. He directed me to Chester McQuarry, manager of an electrical company on US 84.

I followed the mailman's directions and met Chester, a heavyset gray-haired man maybe in his fifties who seemed interested in what I was doing. He was leaving for lunch and invited me to join him. We went to a little café nearby and, on entering, Chester noticed a young man seated alone on the other side of the room. Chester led the way and introduced me to Red, a tall, red-headed electrician.

After complaining about the diet his doctor wanted him to follow, Chester ordered a good sized meal and explained that his father had kept Catahoulas and used them to hunt woods hogs. Many of the woods hogs, Chester said, belonged to his father. The feral woods hogs, which had roamed the woods for over a hundred years, were still the property of many of the men in the parish.

The practice of setting livestock free to find their own sustenance was known as "open range," and was once widely practiced with cattle as well as hogs. When I asked how they could tell which hogs were theirs, Chester explained that the hogs were marked by a pattern cut in one or both ears. The marks were all registered in the parish courthouse. A napkin drawing of his father's mark showed the tip cut off the hog's right ear and two notches in the left (Fig. 2.2). When rounding up their hogs, the hog owners "ear-marked" any unmarked pigs they caught.

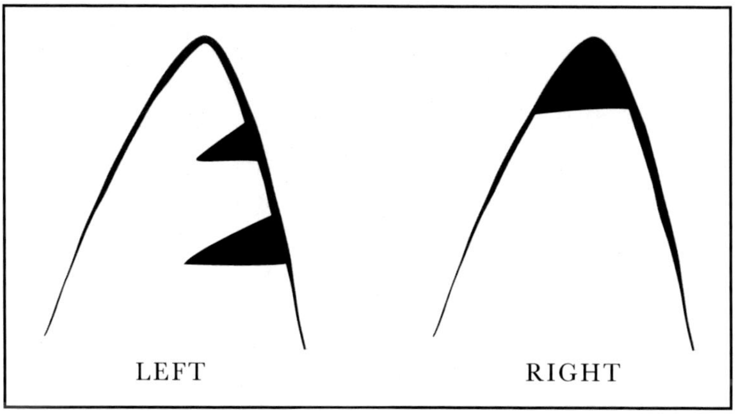

Fig. 2.2 My attempt to copy Chester McQuarry's sketch of his father's ear-mark.

Chester described the dogs, leopard coat, glass eyes, and all. The glass eyes, he said, sometimes included a brown "crack" in the white iris (Fig. In-3). He explained that most litters included some pups who weren't leopards, and they might be any ordinary dog color.

He also described the way Catahoulas caught a hog: one on each side of the head, as I had seen with the Gravel brothers. Each dog grabbed an ear of jowl, Chester said, and held on until the hunters caught up. That's why, he said, Catahoulas are considered "hold" dogs. He hadn't had any experience with Catahoulas in years, not since his dad died, but suggested I talk with Charlie Davis, as ex-game warden who knew a lot about Catahoulas.

During the meal, Chester had been talking, and I had been taking notes, but Red hadn't said two words. Red, Chester said, had hunted hogs and could tell me about it if he weren't so busy ogling the waitress.

I followed Chester's directions to Charlie Davis' double wide trailer a mile or so off the highway. Charlie, a short stocky man was cutting grass when I pulled up. Chester had called to tell him I was coming. Charlie had three Catahoulas, all blue leopards, light gray with black splotches. Two were young males, the other a female Charlie said was about fourteen years old. The old girl was white in the face, and Charlie said she had only one tooth in her mouth.

Hoping to add to what I had learned, I enquired about the origin of the Catahoula. Charlie knew the legend about DeSoto's war dogs, but didn't put much stock in it. He also knew that some people included red wolf in the Catahoula's ancestry, but Catahoulas, he said were nothing like wolves. Charlie reminded me that the Catahoula was a "cur." I remembered Emmit, a friend from my teen years, telling me that the Catahoula was a cur, and that his father's family, in rural St. Tammany Parish, owned several.

The Merriam-Webster Dictionary says a cur is a mongrel or inferior dog. Charlie said a cur was a good stock and hunting dog. He claimed there were several kinds of curs, the Catahoula was one, the black mouth cur another. Black mouth curs, according to Charlie, could be found in southwest Mississippi. He had also heard of a cur dog in Texas, but didn't remember the name. I was pleasantly surprised when Charlie invited me to go hog hunting with him the following Saturday.

That Saturday I arrived at Charlie's as the sun was coming up. My boots were wet with dew from the grass as Charlie, his three dogs and I, got into an old Army surplus jeep he had painted red. We headed down a white shell road while Charlie explained that he was driving slowly because the jeep had no brakes. I checked for my seat belt, but there was none. Great! No brakes and no seat belt in an open jeep.

Charlie assured me there would be no other traffic on this old road.

The road followed what passes for a ridge in South Louisiana, with an elevation of less than two feet, probably an old natural levee. Around us were hardwood trees, including many oaks. I took this as a good sign. Acorns are a favorite food of hogs. Where the ridge had been cleared, I could see cypress on lower, wetter land in the distance.

When we passed a small herd of cattle in a field on our right, one of Charlie's Catahoulas jumped out, hit the hard shell road on his back, leaped up and ran toward the cattle. Charlie didn't slow down or even turn his head.

Puzzled, I said, "Charlie, one of your dogs jumped out."

Charlie replied, "That's okay, he'll be along." When the other two dogs jumped out, each landing with a thud that would have incapacitated most dogs or people, Charlie reassured me: "Yeah, they're tough little boogers. They'll round up those cattle into a tight little bunch and then catch up to us."

Well, Charlie had more faith in his dogs than I did. He continued driving slowly along, not even looking back. Fearing I'd seen the last of Charlie's Catahoulas, I turned and watched in amazement as they gathered the cattle into a small group. The dogs moved the cattle by barking, not at their heels as I had expected, but at their heads (Fig. 2.3). Charlie explained that many stock dogs are heelers—one is even named the Australian blue heeler—but the Catahoula and probably other cur dogs are headers, turning an animal by barking at its head.

Just as Charlie had predicted, once the cattle had been gathered, the dogs came running after us. I expected Charlie to stop (coast to a stop, I guess, we had no brakes) and corral the dogs back into the jeep. Instead, he kept driving slowly along, the dogs trotting alongside, until the old female started lagging behind. We did coast to a stop then, Charlie called the dogs back into the jeep, and we resumed our slow ride.

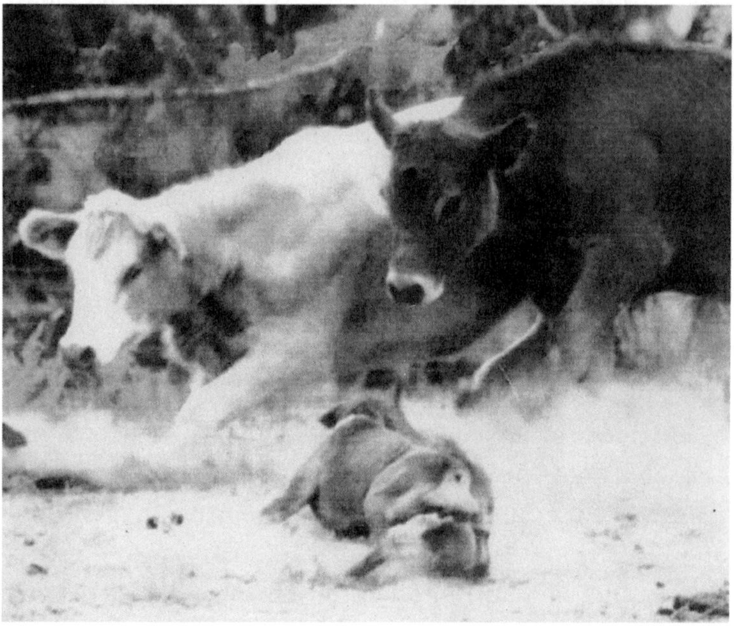

Fig. 2.3 Whether hunting or herding, Catahoulas approach toward the head. Some stockdogs are "heelers." Catahoulas are "headers." Image courtesy of Linda McKay.

We stopped in an area where fresh hog scat dotted the white shell road. Charlie put the dogs out, got back behind the wheel, and with the dogs trotting alongside, started yelling "yuh yuh yuh." Now I'll admit that's the weirdest command I've ever heard anyone give a dog—but what amazed me was its similarity to something I'd read in the LSU library. Around the time of the American Revolution, settlers were moving across the Appalachians. The mountains presented a formidable barrier, given the modes of transportation then used, but there are gaps in the chain of mountains. Gaps through which a stream flows are called "water gaps" and those without streams "wind gaps." Near Asheville, North Carolina, is a water gap through which the French Broad River flows. Pioneers near the western end of the gap, in what is now Tennessee, gathered their hogs from the woods once a year and, with the help of dogs, drove the hogs through the gap to market near Asheville. In my library research, I had come across an article in *Agricultural History*[15] entitled "The Hog Driver's Play Song and Some of its Relatives." The hog drivers encouraged their dogs to move the hogs with the command "yuh yuh yuh," the same command Charlie used. Years later, I read the *Foxfire* series of books. They consist mostly of interviews of elderly people living in northern Georgia's Appalachians. One elderly man, Simmie Free, is quoted as saying that when he was young, hunters would yell the similar "hyah hyah now" to encourage the dogs to hunt hogs.[16] Could there be a connection between eighteenth century Appalachian hog drives and twentieth century hog hunting in Louisiana?

The feral hogs, the dogs used to work them, commands given, methods of hunting, driving, or penning hogs are all items in a cultural complex. Often these cultural complexes travel with people who use them. I took the identical commands, one used on hog drives in the Appalachians, and one used in Catahoula Parish, Louisiana, as a small clue to the origin of the Catahoula.

15 Edmund Cody Burnett. "Hog Raising and Hog Driving in the Region of the French Broad River" Agricultural History Vol. 20 No. 2. 1946

16 Eliot Wigginton. *Foxfire 3*. Knopf Doubleday Publishing Group. New York 1975.

As my mind turned over this exciting new possibility, Charlie's dogs entered the woods. Charlie suggested we wait by the jeep until we heard the dogs. Ten, twenty minutes passed. I wondered whether the dogs were lost, Charlie assured me they were not. He reminded me that Catahoulas, being curs, were silent on trail. If they had been hounds, he said, we'd hear them baying the whole time they were on trail. Coon hunters, Charlie explained, liked nothing better than to wait by their pickup trucks on cold winter nights and listen to the "music of the hounds." When his dogs found a hog, Charlie said, "we'll hear plenty."

Well, that day, Charlie's dogs found no hogs. We heard nothing from for at least an hour before they came back to the jeep. Charlie was disappointed that I hadn't seen his dogs in action. He gave me a pair of tusks he had taken from a boar, as if for a token of consolation. The time we waited by the jeep wasn't wasted, however. Charlie proved quite knowledgeable. I was glad Chester had put me on to him. Charlie explained that Catahoulas are "headers," that is, they approach from the head whether herding, as we'd seen with the cattle, or hunting hogs. His description of Catahoulas catching, grabbing, and holding a hog agreed with what I had seen with the Gravel brothers, and with what Chester McQuarry had described over lunch.

Another distinction between hounds and curs, according to Charlie, is that hounds have "cold" noses and can follow cold trails, which is why they hunt with their noses to the ground, searching for the scent of their quarry. Curs, on the other hand, have "hot" noses, and can follow a scent trail only if it's fresh (hot). As the Gravels' dogs had done, curs hunt with their heads up, as if trying to catch a scent in the wind.

Charlie also described another service performed by Catahoulas: penning hogs.

Back a few decades, hog owners sometimes wanted to pen a number of hogs rather than catch just one. Before the levees were built, when the river was high, the flood plain often flooded except for the natural levees along the streams. Hogs were concentrated on the higher land, and men of the community used Catahoulas to pen the hogs. They built a pen, usually on the bank of a river or bayou so the hogs could be loaded by boat. (I remember a place on the Pearl River that is still called "Hog Pen Point.")

From the pen's gate they built two long wings, or fences, to funnel the hogs into the pen. When penning, the Catahoulas don't try to hold the hogs. Instead the dogs are trained to rile 'em. A fully grown boar, armed with razor-sharp tusks, feeding in the woods with his sow and pigs, will not be chased off by a couple of dogs half his size. When the assaults of the dogs have angered him enough (easy to do), the boar, followed by his sow and pigs, will chase the dogs, and the dogs will run toward the pen. If the boar loses interest, a little barking or a well-placed nip will get him into the chase again. The boar, followed by his herd, will chase the dogs right into the pen. Once they're in, the men close the gate, the dogs jump out, and the hogs are penned.

Another quote from Leak Bevil backs Charlie's account:

> He'd [the cur] get the animal to fightin' 'im and then he'd run from it, and he'd come back and get the animal to fightin' 'im again and keep runnin' till he got that bunch of hogs to follow 'im. When he got to the pen where you wanted to pen 'em, he went in the gate and they just followed right on in, and he'd jump out the other side and you'd close the gate.[17]

17 Campbell and Lynn Loughmiller. *The Big Thicket Legacy*. University of Texas Press. Austin. 1977.

Though my hog hunt with Charlie had bagged no hogs, Charlie's remarkable knowledge about Catahoulas, and curs in general, inspired me to learn more. The most surprising thing Charlie said was in response to my question about the value of a good Catahoula. He claimed that most of the people in the area thought it not just wrong, but sinful, to sell a dog. I said something corny about dogs being priceless, but Charlie swore that somewhere in the Bible is an admonition against selling dogs. I made a mental note to find out more about this.

Almost a week later, I stopped for gas near Dry Prong, Louisiana. A young man in neatly pressed slacks and a short-sleeved white shirt approached the car next to mine, identified himself as a Christian missionary and asked the lady driving whether she'd been saved. I was half-way hoping I could get my gas and leave before the missionary came to my car, but no such luck.

He walked over to me and asked, "What about you friend, have you been saved?"

Before I answered, I remembered what Charlie Davis had said about the Bible forbidding the sale of dogs. When I asked about it, the missionary beamed, seemingly pleased that he could display his biblical knowledge.

He responded with a quote: "Thou shall not bring the hire of a whore or the price of a dog into the house of the Lord." He told me to check Deuteronomy chapter 22 or 23. Check it I did, and Deuteronomy 23, verse 18 (King James version) says: "Thou shall not bring the hire of a whore or the price of a dog into the house of the Lord, thy God, for any vow: for even both these are an abomination unto the Lord, thy God." Apparently the young missionary—and Charlie Davis—knew their Bible!

Back in Baton Rouge, I went over what I had learned. The Catahoula was apparently an important part of culture in the Catahoula area. It helped provide pork, and when penned hogs were loaded onto boats, the hogs could be sold.

I had learned that the Catahoula was a cur, a special kind of dog with particular talents. They could hold an animal, giving hunters time to arrive, and could pen hogs and even herd cattle. I had learned that there were other kinds of curs, the black mouth cur in Mississippi, probably one in Texas, and I suspected the dogs that drove hogs along the French Broad were curs. What I still didn't know was where curs came from.

I was pondering my next step when a classmate, Frank Wood, told me he had seen Catahoula-like dogs in Livingston Parish, just south of the recently built I-12 highway. Livingston Parish isn't in the flood plain; in fact, it's on the opposite side of the Mississippi River. I had associated the Catahoula with the flood plain, where Catahoula Lake and Catahoula Parish are, but maybe Frank's sighting was worth checking out.

On the next day, I drove to Livingston and through the area Frank had seen the dogs. Driving through piney woods, I noticed, in back of a small trailer, a hog carcass hung over a kettle of water. The kettle was of the type once used to boil down cane juice on Louisiana sugar plantations. The residents of this trailer had found a new use for it.

When I stopped my car, two dogs, one obviously a Catahoula leopard, seemed determined that I not get out of my car. I tried opening my window to talk to the dogs and try to calm them down, but when the larger dog tried to jump through the window at me, I decided it might be best to wait. Eventually, a tall dark-haired man exited the trailer and hushed the dogs. I explained what I was doing, and he boasted that I was looking at two of the best hog dogs in Louisiana. I didn't doubt it; after all, the evidence was hanging over the kettle.

As I got out of the car, Roy Watson introduced himself and his dogs. Roy's leopard was named Sidekick, and the smaller dog, Brownie, was Sidekick's mother. Roy explained that Sidekick's father had been a leopard. Sidekick had been one of two leopards in a litter of six. Every litter, according to Roy, included some non-leopards, even if both parents were leopards. Sidekick was a blue leopard, a little bigger than Charlie Davis' dogs and had a hole in his abdomen where a hog had gored him. Roy explained he had stitched the hole closed, but that Sidekick had pulled out the stitches. Brownie, Sidekick's mother, was a smaller dog, brown with a little black.

Roy said he and a friend were going hog hunting in the morning, as there were some unmarked shoats in the woods, and he wanted to put his mark on them. When I asked what a shoat was, Roy gave me a condescending look, but explained that a shoat was a half-grown pig. I asked if I could come to watch and maybe take some pictures. Roy thought I'd have trouble keeping up. "When we hear them dogs, we got to move!" What it was that made Roy think I couldn't keep up, I don't know. I was in my twenties and in good physical condition.

Eventually he agreed to let me come. "Well, if you can't keep up with me, try to keep up with my buddy."

I got to Roy's trailer as the rising sun was chasing the mist from the pines. Compared to parishes on the flood plain, Livingston is a little higher, the soil is sandy and lighter in color, and the vegetation is completely different. The flood plain supports a hardwood forest, but here in Livingston, ninety percent of the trees around me were pines. The important thing though, was that Livingston had feral hogs and Catahoula hog dogs.

When Roy opened the door, he and a young man with a crew cut were finishing cups of coffee. I was introduced to Frizell Bobbins, who worked with Roy in Baton Rouge. Roy offered me some coffee. I said I'd appreciate some, but he replied, "You'll have to drink up, you're makin' us late." I declined the coffee. Roy wasn't the most congenial guy in the parish!

When we began the hunt, I saw why Roy thought I might not be able to keep up with him: he mounted a horse, leaving Frizell and me on foot! This time we didn't stay on the road and wait to hear the dogs. Instead we entered the woods and tried to stay as close to the dogs as we could. We started our hunt on abandoned farmland where we could still make out furrows in the ground, although the field now supported pines over ten feet tall.

Ahead of us the dogs spotted an armadillo. What happened next I wouldn't believe if I hadn't seen it. The armadillo didn't run. It dug! Soil flew every which way and the armadillo sank into the ground! I'm sure the soft, furrowed ground aided its escape, along with the fact that the dogs couldn't sink their teeth into its armor, but seeing an animal disappear straight downward is a sight I won't forget.

After the armadillo incident, the Catahoulas continued their silent hunt. Twenty or thirty minutes later, I was beginning to suspect another unsuccessful hunt when all hell broke loose. Near a creek, a hundred yards to our left, was a commotion that meant the dogs had found something. We all took off, Roy ahead of us on his horse. I caught up just in time to see him dive off his horse and grab a half-grown pig. He yelled at his dogs to back off as he straddled the shoat.

Roy drew a knife and cut two notches in each of the shoat's ears. "Okay!" Roy yelled, "This one's mine!"

Later that morning, Roy's dogs caught another shoat, this time in a patch of palmettos. When I reached them, just as Charlie Davis had predicted, each dog had the squealing shoat by an ear. After Roy marked and released this shoat, he explained, as Charlie had, that Catahoulas are "hold" dogs, capable of catching and holding a hog by the ears or jowls until the hunter catches up.

Roy agreed with Charlie about Catahoulas' hot noses, even claiming Catahoulas' hunting tactics were superior to scent hounds' ability to follow cold trails. "Guys who hunt with hounds sometimes lose their dogs, because hounds, with their cold noses, follow trails that go to hell and back. When the hound finally gets back to where the hunt started (sometimes after a day or two) the hunter may be long gone."[18]

The two shoats were the only swine caught that day, and true to form, Roy's dogs had "given voice" only when they had caught the shoats. I hadn't expected them to have the drawl of a hound, but I noticed they had slightly high-pitched voices for dogs their size.

The hunt with Roy Watson and his dogs reminded of a story I had read in high school. In *The Bear*,[19] the great Mississippi writer, William Faulkner tells about Lion, a dog he doesn't describe as a cur, but whose hunting behavior matched what I had witnessed and been told about curs.

Faulkner writes of Old Ben, a very large, wise, and dangerous bear. Old Ben had been pursued for years by a group of area hunters and their pack of scent hounds. It's beginning to look like they'll never get Old Ben when Lion enters the scene from parts unknown. Sam Fathers, father figure

18 Field Notes, May 19659.

19 William Faulkner. "The Bear" Big Woods:-The Hunting Stories. New York: Random House. 1955.

to the protagonist, captures and tames Lion and proclaims that Lion is the dog that is "gonter hold Old Ben."

Later in the narrative, the protagonist, listening to the dogs on Old Ben's trail, concludes that Lion isn't among them. He hears the drawl of the hounds, but not the distinctive voice of Lion. Sam tells him that Lion is, indeed with the pack, but that Lion would never "cry on trail," but that once Lion catches Old Ben, "you'll hear him plenty." This is exactly the behavior of a cur. Sam's remarks closely echo Charlie Davis' commentary on his own dogs' tactics.

Before the final hunt, on an especially cold December day, the protagonist worries that the cold would prevent the dogs from detecting Old Ben's trail. Sam Fathers reminds him that unlike a scent hound, "Lion don't need no nose. All he need is a bear." Just as I had learned about curs, Lion has a hot nose.

When the cold-nosed hounds find Old Ben, they hang back, intimidated by the formidable bear. Only one hound joins in as Lion attacks Old Ben, going for the throat and holding on. Again, in behavior typical of curs, Lion grabs his quarry near the head. Charlie Davis once said that curs were the bravest of dogs. I don't know whether Lion was brave or foolhardy, but he certainly attacked a very large bear and survived.

As far as I know, William Faulkner wasn't a hunter. He is known for writing about the people and times he knew. Faulkner's knowledge about cur behavior may have been second hand, but he got it right!

I had been on hunts using curs. Though Lion is the only cur in Faulkner's narrative, the other dogs being hounds, hunting with hounds and curs was once common in the South. The hounds, with their superior sense of smell, were used to find the quarry. When the hounds had bayed the animal, the curs were released to hold the animal for the hunters. An 1851 edition of *De Bow's Review* described an actual bear hunt with hounds and curs. It took place on Sicily Island, in Catahoula Parish.[20] The hounds were used to find the bear. Curs were sent in to keep the bear from running. The consistency between what my research was turning up and Faulkner's story was encouraging, even if the origins of the Catahoula remained elusive.

My conversations with people in the field and my experience hunting hogs, taught me a lot about the physical and behavioral characteristics of the Catahoula. By now I was thoroughly impressed by the Catahoula and by curs in general. I decided that my next step should be to examine breeds with similar characteristics, possibly finding a clue to the Catahoula's ancestry that way.

---

20 A. R. Kilpatrick. "Early Life in the Southwest" De Bow's Review 13:378-383. 1852.

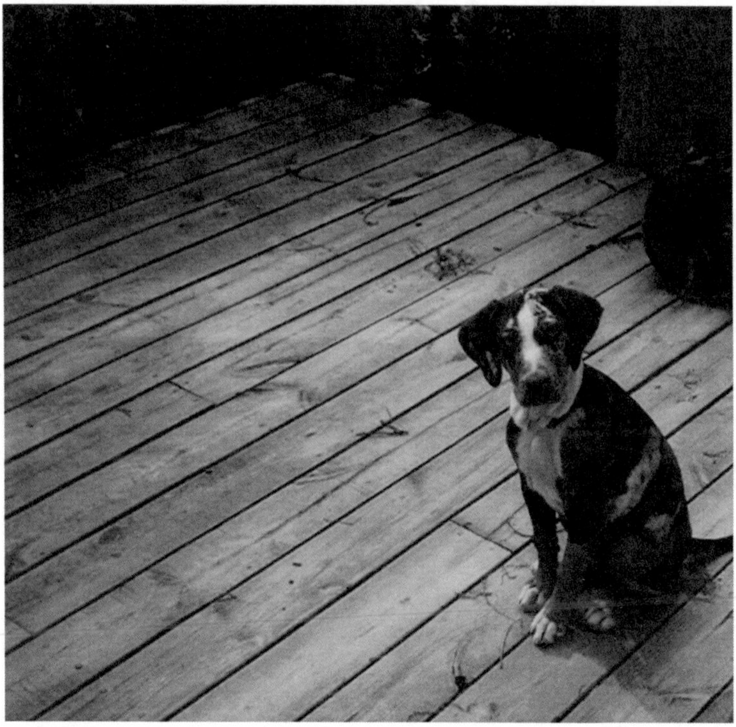

Fig. 2.4 A lonely little red leopard. Image courtesy of Vicki Loudenslager.

CHAPTER THREE
THE SEARCH FOR CATAHOULA ANCESTORS

In my search for the origin of the Catahoula cur, I sought other breeds that shared its characteristics. The most distinctive characteristic of the Catahoula is merling, usually with accompanying glass eyes (eyes with white irises). I wanted to learn which other breeds shared this characteristic. I knew that not all Catahoulas were merled. Chester McQuarry, among others, had said that every litter, even if both parents are merled, included some pups that were not merled and some pups that were mostly white. The mostly white offspring were likely to have poor hearing and vision. I'll call these "double merles." I suspected that other breeds that exhibited merling might be ancestors or related to the Catahoula.

I found four other kinds of dogs that included merled individuals. They are: 1) collies and their kin, the Shetland sheepdog, the border collie, the Australian shepherd, etc. (Fig. 3.1) 2) some breeds of scent hounds, including the Norwegian dunker harrier, the English harrier, and the dachshund 3) the Beauceron, a French sheepdog, and 4) the Great Dane.

THE COLLIE CONNECTION

The collie breeds are descended from the border collie, which is probably named for the England-Scotland border country where sheep continue to be raised and border collies

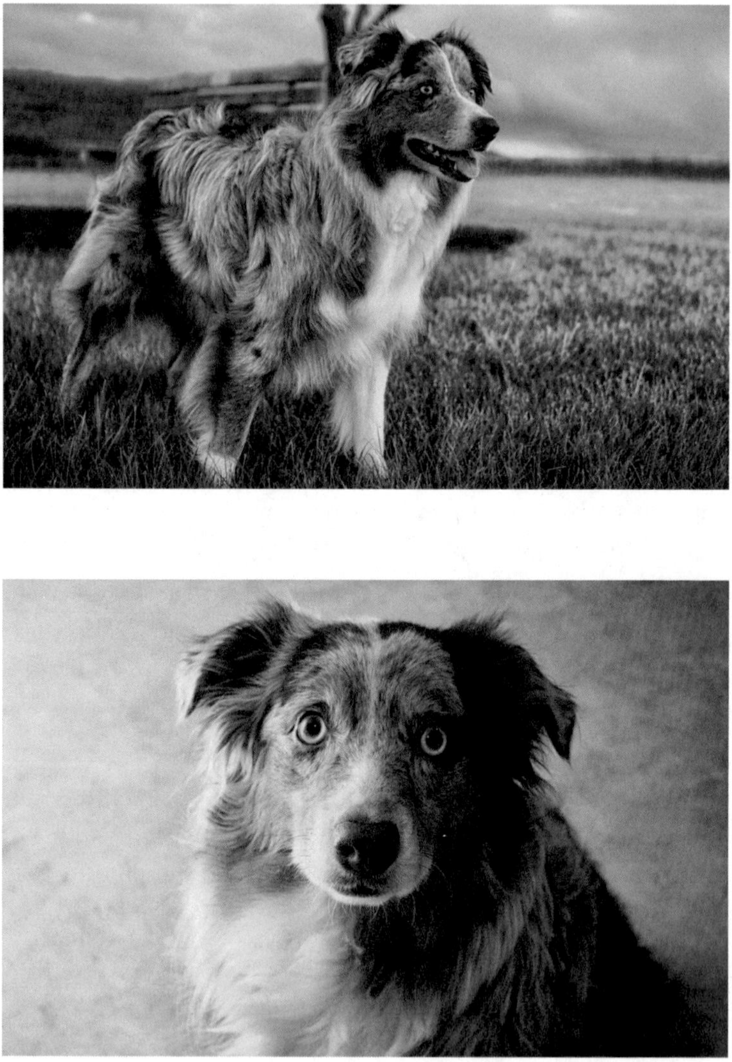

Fig. 3.1 Merled Australian shepherds. Members of the collie group.. Images courtesy of Ted Van Pelt, flic.kr/p/pNeiu2; flic.kr/p/nUgXjs.

are still used. Like the border collie, Catahoulas are often used to herd livestock. Maybe, I thought, the two are related.

At a feed store I came across a homemade magazine[21] that included an announcement of stockdog trials to be held at Stodghill's Ranch in Quinlan, TX. The announcement said the trials would include both border collies and Catahoulas. This, I thought, is the perfect chance to compare the two breeds. I was able to get in touch with Tom Stodghill by phone, and he assured me I'd be welcome. He said Catahoulas were known in Texas in addition to another cur breed, the lacy. Both breeds, Tom said, worked in the same way, both being hold dogs, holding hogs by the ears. Early in the summer of 1969, I set out with a photographer friend, Perry Torregano, for Quinlan.

We met Tom Stodgill early in the morning on the day of the trials. Tom was the picture of the Texas rancher. He stood a good six feet tall, wore a western hat, and sported a big shiny western belt buckle. Tom had recognized, years ago, the uniqueness of the Catahoula. He had started a registry, the Animal Research Foundation, to preserve the Catahoula and other folk breeds of dogs, cattle and hogs from possible extinction. This was the first formal registry for the Catahoula.

Tom led Perry and me to a huge fenced field where the trials would take place. Within the field was a ten or twelve-foot square enclosure made with split-rail fencing. One entire side could open as a gate. Fifty or sixty yards from the pen, forming a triangle with the pen, were two sets of fencing, each with an opening of eight to ten feet. These "gates" simply provided openings for the sheep to be driven through. Tom emphasized that the sheep were "wild," that is, had never before been herded. Each dog would work

21 *Stodghill's Animal Research Magazine.* winter, 1968.

with five sheep. The rules called for the dog to be cast (sent in a large circle to the rear of the flock), collect the sheep, drive them through gate number one, gate number two, and into the pen—all within fifteen minutes! (Fig. 3.2) The dog would be directed by its handler, who used spoken or whistled commands.

When I asked whether Catahoulas and border collies were going to compete against each other, Tom replied, "No. Border collies are going to herd sheep. Catahoulas would *kill* sheep." He explained that Catahoulas are good for working hogs or cattle, but are "too damn rough" to use on sheep. A contestant I spoke with later thought it was a matter of training. Sure, he said, a Catahoula unfamiliar with sheep might attack one, just as he might attack a possum or raccoon, but some Catahoulas are the playmates and guardians of young children. He knew of a Catahoula used to herd turkeys and had never hurt one. Another man had a Catahoula that slept under a tree in which his hens slept. Foxes and bobcats abounded in the area, and it might've seemed safer to lock the chickens up, but the man said, "As long as that cur sleeps under that tree, my chickens are safer than they'd be in a coop."

Tom thought Catahoulas too rough for sheep, but border collies, he said, are the ballet dancers of the stock dog world. Perry asked what he meant by that, and Tom replied, "Beauty and precision. They do their job with beauty and precision." I was anxious to see border collies perform.

Later, as the trials proceeded, I saw what Tom meant. A border collie and his handler entered the field, and the handler cast his dog around the flock. Once the dog was in what the handler thought was an effective position, the handler whistled, and the dog dropped to the ground. On command, the dog rose and walked slowly toward the sheep.

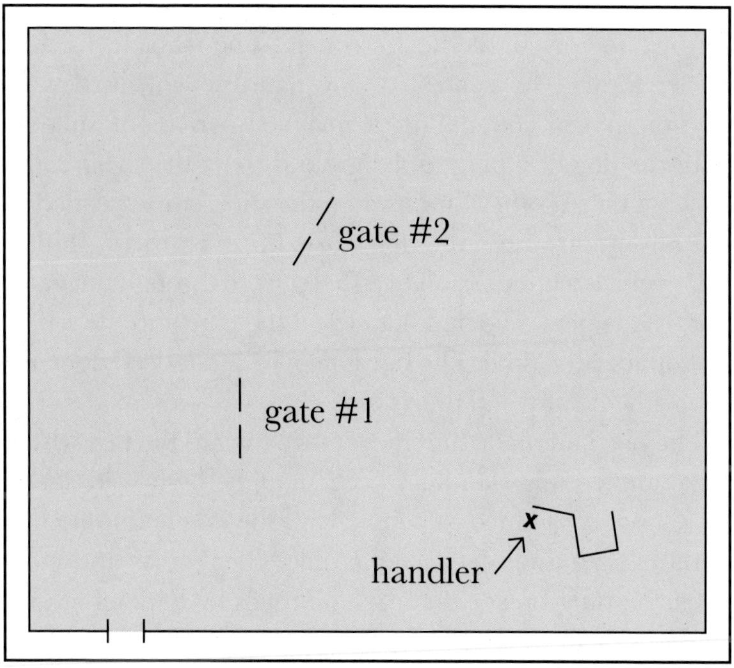

Fig. 3.2 Plan of the field used in sheep dog trials at Stodghill's Ranch. Not to scale.

1. The dog enters the field and his handler "casts" him. (He runs around to the rear of the sheep in a wide arc.)

2. "Gates" 1 and 2 each consist of two lengths of fencing set six feet apart. The dog must drive the sheep through gate #1 then gate #2.

3. The dog must drive the sheep into the ten-foot square pen and keep them in while the handler closes the hinged side.

4. The time elapsed between the dog's entry into the field and the closing of the pen is announced.

The sheep moved away from the dog, toward gate #1. Often, the sheep tried to turn; each time the dog positioned himself to correct the flock's course. The whole drive was under the careful control of the handler, who used whistled or spoken commands. It involved periods of stillness, with the dog dropping to the ground to let the sheep settle down a bit. At other times, when the sheep were headed in the wrong direction, the dog rushed to turn them. Within relatively few minutes, all five sheep were through the gates and in the pen. The handler closed the gate and the scorer announced the time. The border collie had indeed done his job with "beauty and precision."

The dog had made the sheep move toward the pen where the handler was standing, even though these wild sheep were not accustomed to people, and the dog had to do this without scattering the sheep. Unlike Catahoulas and most other herding breeds that drive animals by barking at and nipping them, border collies move sheep by simply being in the right place at the right time. A difficult task, but they were enthusiastic about their work. The dogs were visibly anxious to perform.

The border collie next up was too aggressive. He moved in on the sheep too quickly, and they scattered. Precious time was lost as the dog rounded up the sheep again. I was standing among a group of sheep men at the time, and the preponderance of opinion was that the handler, not the dog, was at fault. Another border collie walked slowly toward the sheep, intending to intimidate them into moving, but one sheep, braver than the others, faced the dog and wouldn't move. The sheep stood his ground until dog and sheep actually touched noses—at which point the dog was disqualified because he had touched a sheep.

Earlier, I had wandered through the area where the sheep dog handlers had set up. Their pickups bore licenses from several midwestern and southwestern states. Some had small trailers. All of the dogs I saw were border collies. Almost all were black and white, but a few had some sable on their faces. None of them were merled. Their hair was longer than that of a Catahoula, but nowhere near as long as that of the dog we think of as a collie.

An Ohio dog named Penny was the winner of the trials. I had seen Penny and another border collie by their owner's pickup that morning. Each dog was in a crate with an open side. The crates were in the shade of a live oak, out of the summer heat. Each dog had water and a piece of carpet to lie on. They weren't tied or restrained in any way, yet each stayed by his crate. The handler was about fifty yards away, seemingly not paying any attention to his dogs. When it was time for one of his dogs to compete, the handler whistled and only that dog came running, eager to show his stuff. After the dog panned the sheep, the handler patted the dog, sent it back to its crate, and whistled for the other dog. The dogs were beautifully trained and performed exquisitely.

The Catahoula event at the trials was not a competition; it was a demonstration. A 250-pound sow was let loose in the field after the sheep were taken off. Although she was a sow, not a boar, she had razor-sharp tusks that looked to be two or three inches long. Two men in a pickup with two Catahoulas in back drove onto the field. The Catahoulas were set free and immediately ran for the sow. The hog was fast, but no match for the dogs. One dog, coming up on her right, grabbed her jowl. When she turned to gore him, he let go and dodged. A moment later, both dogs were on the hog, one on each side. When she turned on the dog on her right, the one on her left yanked on her jowl. When she turned on the dog on her left, the dog on her right did the same.

Eventually the hog, although continually complaining, stood still between the dogs that, together, were less than half her weight. The men drove up and somehow got a rope around one on the hog's hind legs. The dogs were told to let go. With the men pulling the rope and the dogs driving, the hog was forced up a ramp and into the back of the pickup. The Catahoulas had demonstrated their talent. The question of elegance aside, they had done what no dog but a cur could do.

Clearly, the styles of the border collies and Catahoulas were very different. Border collies worked with constant instruction from their handler. Catahoulas, after the "yuh yuh yuh" command were on their own until they caught a hog and the hunters caught up. The border collies had compelled the sheep to move simply by their presence; the Catahoulas had chased and then grabbed the hog. What part does training play in these differences in behavior?

Leading French breeder and user of sheep herding dogs, Sabine Ehlers, has learned that, in regard to behaviors, only the simplest (instincts) were inherited. More complex behaviors had to be taught, but some breeds had an inherent aptitude for some tasks. Border collies were trained to follow a complex set of commands. Catahoulas may be trained to follow commands (yuh yuh yuh), but they have an instinct to go for an animal's head area (ear, jowl) and hold on. They instinctively go for the head and hold on. They are headers and hold dogs.

Aptitudes are inherited, specific behaviors are not. If a dog has an aptitude to be a retriever, he will be easier to train for that job. The dog hasn't inherited the behaviors required of a good retriever; all he's inherited is the potential to learn the job more easily than dogs of other breeds.

Another breeder relates observations of cocker spaniel pups from a hunting line. "Whenever a bird or butterfly flitted across the pen," he wrote, "every puppy tried to catch it, dancing, sometimes on hind legs, and rushing around the pen until they came to the wire fence." When observing pointer and English setter puppies (both, like the cocker spaniels, bird dog breeds) in the same situation he got similar results. He then observed bloodhound puppies and bull terrier puppies (not bird dogs). These puppies showed no interest in small flying things whatsoever. Finally, he put all the puppies together in a large pen. He thought that perhaps the bird dog pups would "infect with enthusiasm" the non-bird pups. This was not to be. When sparrows flitted across the pen, the bird dog pups became excited. The non-bird dog pups still did not. Only the bird dog pups had inherited an interest in small flying things. They had the aptitude to become good hunters of birds.[22]

Border collies inherit an aptitude for herding sheep. Curs inherit an aptitude for catching hogs by the ears and holding them. It would be very difficult to train one to do the job of the other. I concluded that it was highly unlikely that the Catahoula could be descended from the border collie.

22 Sabine Ehlers. "How much intelligence is inherited in dogs?" Quora. Accessed 3/17/21. quora.com/How-much intelligence-is-inherited-in-dogs.

COULD THE CATAHOULA BE RELATED TO THE SCENT HOUNDS?

I found three scent hound breeds that included merled dogs: the Norwegian Dunker harrier, the English harrier, and the dachshund. (Fig. 3.4) I wondered whether there could be an ancestral link between these dogs and the Catahoula. As we have seen, during my field research, I met a number of people who used the word "hound" as a synonym for "scent hound," and emphasized the differences between hounds and curs. These are summarized in Table 3.1:

QUALITY	SCENT HOUND	CUR
Use in hunting	Trailing—Finding the quarry	Holding and delaying the quarry until arrival of the hunters
Trailing ability (nose)	Cold nose—can follow a cold scent trail	Hot nose—can follow only a hot or fresh trail
Position of head while hunting	Nose to ground—searching for or following a scent trail	Head up, trying to catch a scent in the wind or sight the quarry
Voice	Drawl	Higher pitched chop
Use of voice while trailing	Bays on trail	Silent until quarry is found
Ear	Pendant, long	Shorter than that of a hound and triangular when viewed from the front

Table 3.1: Scent hound vs. cur characteristics.

Additionally: 1) Curs are herders while hounds are not, and 2) curs can make hogs follow (chase) them into a pen. Hounds cannot do this; I doubt there is any non-cur breed that can. All of these differences between scent hounds and curs show the improbability of the two being closely related.

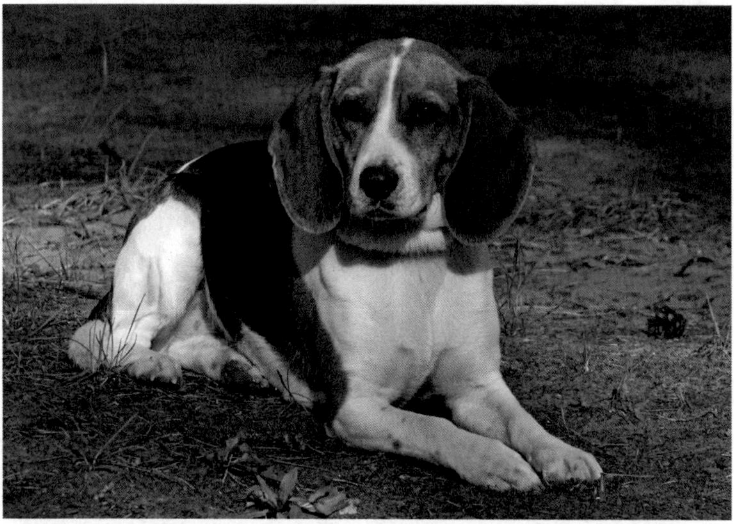

Fig 3.3 Beagle, a typical scent hound. Beagles and foxhounds are among the oldest extant scent hound breeds. Image courtesy of FreeImages.com/Alan Bridges.

COULD THE CATAHOULA BE RELATED TO THE BEAUCERON?

The Beauceron is a French herding dog. (Fig. 3.5) It is slightly larger than the average Catahoula and, although typically black and tan, some Beaucerons are merled. There are some key differences between the Beauceron and the Catahoula. Functionally, the Catahoula is as much a hunting dog as it is a herding dog. The Beauceron is primarily a herder of sheep and cattle. It has been trained for use by the police and military, but I found no references to the Beauceron as a hunter.

There are also a couple of physical traits in which the two breeds differ. All breeds typically have five digits on each paw. Four are functional toes, which can be seen in a paw print. The fifth is called the dew claw and is located a couple of inches above the paw. The Beauceron, however, has two dew claws on each hind leg.[23] It shares this characteristic with one or two other European breeds but not with the Catahoula. Also, historically, a large percentage of Catahoulas have been brindle (some still are), but brindle is not one of the Beauceron's coat patterns.

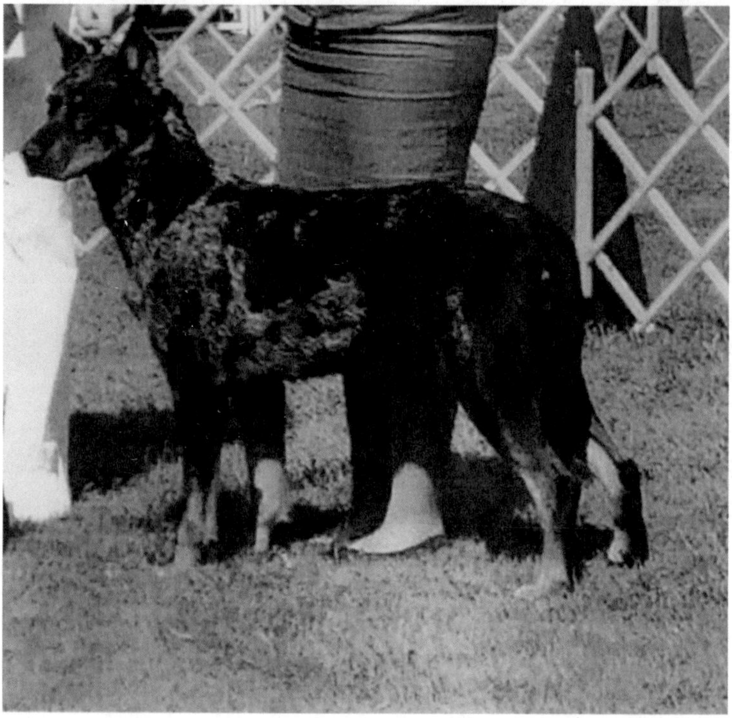

Fig. 3.4 The Beauceron, a French sheep dog, sometimes merled, is from northern France, and isn't associated with Louisiana's Cajun country. Image courtesy of Carol Cossey.

Still, the Beauceron is a French dog, and Louisiana was a French colony. Could they have been brought to Louisiana by French settlers and become ancestors to the Catahoula? The problem with this theory is that neither the Beauce-

23 American Kennel Club. *The New Complete Dog Book.*

ron nor the Catahoula are or have been common in parts of Louisiana settled by French people. Instead, Catahoulas were and are common in northern Louisiana and the Florida Parishes—areas populated by descendants of English-speaking pioneers.

Although there are merled Beaucerons and merled Catahoulas, there are many reasons to conclude that the Beauceron is not the ancestor of the Catahoula.

COULD THE CATAHOULA BE RELATED TO THE GREAT DANE?

The first Great Danes I came across in my research were harlequins, distinguished looking white dogs with black splotches. (Fig. 3.6) Their merling looked so different from that of Catahoulas, I was tempted to assume the Danes weren't merled at all. Merled Catahoulas usually have gray, brown, or reddish-brown background colors. Looking at a harlequin Great Dane, I thought of the Catahoulas I had come to understand were "double Merles." If a Catahoula has one gene for merling, it is merled. If it has two, it is a double merle, its coat is mostly white, and its vision and hearing are likely impaired.[24]

Unlike double merle Catahoulas, however, there is no predisposition for sensory impairment in harlequin Great Danes. Despite their mostly white coats, they aren't double merles; instead, they possess a gene found in some Great Danes, but not in any other breed.[25] This "harlequin gene" is a modifier of merling. Like a popular laundry detergent's motto used to say, it "takes the gray out." Harlequin Great

24 Leon Whitney. *How to Breed Dogs.*

25 Lina Basquette. *How to Raise and Train a Great Dane.*

Danes possess both this special harlequin gene and the gene for merling found in Catahoulas. Their appearance is different from that of merled Catahoulas because the harlequin gene modifies the merling. There are also Great Danes with merling just like that of Catahoula leopards. These Great Danes do not possess the harlequin gene, just the merling gene.

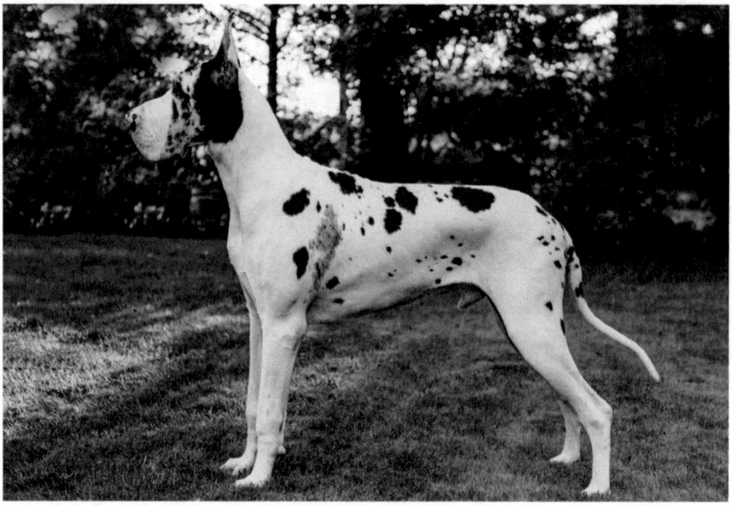

Fig. 3.5 A classic harlequin Great Dane. Despite his name, the Great Dane is not Danish. He's a German dog. Image courtesy of Bill Marquardt.

The Great Dane's ancestors included the boar dog used in the Alps of eighteenth century Germany and Austria. The boar dog, like most ancient breeds (and like the Catahoula), varied a lot physically, but varied little in their determination to catch anything upon which they were loosed. Their muzzles varied from short, boxer-type muzzles (the boxer is also a descendent of the boar dog) to longer, Catahoula-type muzzles. Their weights varied from probably thirty to about one hundred pounds. Boar dog coats were variously colored, but some were brindled and some were merled, both traditional Great Dane and Catahoula coat conditions.

Eventually two sizes of boar dogs came to be recognized: the larger became the ancestor of the Great Dane, and the smaller type became the ancestor of the boxer. The split may have been the result of English mastiff genes added to the Great Dane's ancestral line and English bulldog genes added to the boxer's ancestral line.

When I read that the ancient boar dog was unusual among hunting breeds in that it was trained for "catching and holding game until the arrival of the hunters,"[26] I knew I had a good lead. When the author added that "they hunt small bears and are taught to tackle them at the ears," I was almost ecstatic. That is exactly what Catahoulas do! But how do we get from Austria and southern Germany, where most boar dogs were used, to the Catahoula Lake country?

26 John Wagner. *The Boxer.*

CHAPTER FOUR
HISTORY

I searched history for some connection between the alpine areas of southern Germany and Austria, where boar dogs were used, and the Catahoula Lake area. I learned that before the American Revolution, German-speaking settlers came to the New World in fairly large numbers. Some were Austrian or Swiss, but because they spoke German, to other colonists, they were all Germans.

The newcomers often brought what they needed to feed themselves in the new land. They brought seeds, tools, and sometimes livestock. British settlers, English and Scottish, brought collie-type dogs to herd livestock, scent hounds for hunting, and a little terrier called a feist for rodent control. German settlers brought boar dogs.

The German settlers came to America for a number of reasons. Some sought land of their own. Serfdom was still practiced in Germany, and they were tired of working land belonging to someone else, they wanted land of their own. Many Germans came to America to avoid religious persecution. Some were Quakers or Mennonites, others, during a religious revival in the 1680s had accepted a return to Biblical authority and joined evangelical churches. There were Moravians, members of the Church of the Brethren (called Dunkers because they baptized by immersion), and others.

As early as 1683[27] German Quakers and Mennonites began arriving in Philadelphia and founded Germantown,

27 David W. Young

Pennsylvania. Other Germans arrived in the first decade of the eighteenth century.

In 1965, the Pennsylvania legislature named the Great Dane, a descendent of the boar dog, their state dog partly in honor of the "large dogs" of the German settlers.

Queen Anne of England paid for the passage, from London to New York, of a number of German refugees. These "Poor Palatines," as they were called, because most were from the Palatinate in Germany, were the objects of the Queen's largess, but not entirely because she was altruistic. She wanted to reduce the number of poor people in London. The Poor Palatines settled in the Hudson and Mohawk Valleys in New York.[28]

Queen Anne died in 1714, leaving no surviving offspring. Even after the queen's death, German settlers were welcomed in English colonies. The English had turned, for a monarch, to Anne's German cousin, who became George I of England. George was of the House of Hanover and was never comfortable with English, German remained his language all his life. Under the rule of George and his Hanoverian successors, German settlers were welcomed colonists.

In 1710, other settlers from the Palatinate joined German-speaking Swiss to found New Bern, in North Carolina. In 1719, more Dunkers [no kin to the Dunker harrier] arrived in Philadelphia. By 1727, there were twenty thousand Germans in Pennsylvania, Maryland, and Virginia. In Pennsylvania, the Germans were called "Pennsylvania Deutsch." (The German word for German is Deutsch.) The term was later corrupted to "Pennsylvania Dutch."

The Dunkers, and many other German immigrants, brought with them the seeds and animals needed to make a living in the New World. Their boar dogs had been success-

28 H. T. Dickinson

ful in hunting wild swine and bear in Europe. They were also adept at herding hogs and cattle. The settlers would find them very useful in the New World.

In1735, two years after colonists under James Oglethorpe founded Georgia, a group of German-speaking evangelical Protestants arrived and built a settlement they called Ebenezer. They had emigrated from the area of Salzburg, Austria (boar dog country) and nearby parts of Germany and Switzerland. Their English neighbors practiced "open range." They simply turned their hogs and cattle loose to find food. Later, many of the Germans would adopt this practice. By 1741 there were one thousand two hundred Salzburgers in Georgia. They had built the settlements of Bethany and Goshen. In neighboring North Carolina, German settlers were prospering. A 1742 record shows that one farmer owned 27 horses, 75 head of cattle, and 200 hogs.

There were certainly boar dogs in America before 1750, but to my knowledge, the earliest record that calls them boar dogs is from 1750.[29] In that year, a German named Johannes Plott brought his family and his pack of boar dogs to North Carolina. Some of Plott's dogs were black, and some were brindle (both typical Catahoula colors). Johannes Plott and his family were very proud of the hunting ability of their boar dogs, and were constantly trying to improve their strain. In 1780, Montraville Plott, grandson of Johannes, mated some of their dogs with a "spotted leopard bear dog" owned by a hunter from Rabun Gap, Georgia.[30] As a result, some of the dogs in Plott's pack were leopards.

This "spotted leopard bear dog" must have been related to Salzburger's boar dog. The boar dog was traditionally used on bear in Europe. In fact, he was often called the

29 Bob Plott

30 Ansley-Herring Wegener

"barenbeiser" (German: bear biter). Hence the term "bear dog." The appellation "leopard" has been used to describe merled dogs like the Louisiana Catahoula leopard dog, which, as I discovered, is a descendant of the boar dog.

Plott's dogs later came to be called Plott curs. Today they're called Plott hounds. Some of the Plott men were disappointed that some of Montraville's Plott curs were leopard dogs (a result of spotted leopard bear dog matings). The dogs Johannes had brought from Germany were black or brindle, and the more change-resistant of Montraville's relatives thought that Plott curs should be black or brindle. They persuaded Montraville to give away his leopard dogs. Today, none of the descendants of Plott's dogs are merled.

Von (or Vaughn) Plott, Montraville's son, preferred a cold-nosed dog (a better trailer) to those of his family. The Plott cur could catch and hold a hog or bear if they found one, but scent hounds were better at trailing and finding game. Von reportedly crossed the Plott cur with a scent hound, creating the long-eared Plott hound. It may have been at this time that the name change from Plott cur to Plott hound occurred.

Two types of Plott hound descended from Plott's pack, the long-eared Plott hound and the short-eared Plott hound. Both are still popular among hunters. Philip Rice and John Dahl, in their book, *Hunting Dogs*, express the opinion that the long-eared Plott was the original type brought from Germany. My experience with Catahoulas, and my reading on the subject, convinces me otherwise. The short-eared Plott, as the following quote from Rice and Dahl indicates, has the features of the boar dog (and those of the cur):

> The shorter-eared hounds are, however, possessed of greater speed, and are usually more efficient and evasive fighters on such game as wild boar and bear. For this reason, the shorter-eared variety is usually preferred by most hunters of those animals. The longer-eared type usually has better voice [more like a scent hound's]. Bad voice is usually characteristic of the short-eared type, which usually do not have excellent cold-trailing abilities, and are less open on trail.[31]

The short-eared Plott was, according to Rice and Dahl, an "efficient and evasive fighter" with "bad voice" like the boar dog and cur. The long-eared Plott, with his "excellent cold-trailing abilities, better voice (this may be in the ear of the beholder) and "openness on trail," shares these characteristics with scent hounds. The long-eared Plott is part scent hound.

The Germans brought the boar dog, or the cur, as he came to be called, to America, to the British colonies on the Atlantic, but the story would be incomplete without mention of another people, the Scotch-Irish. (Outside of America they're called the Scots-Irish.)

By the seventeenth century, the English had conquered Ireland, but the restive Irish were always trying to rid themselves of their English overlords. In 1609, the English decided to settle some loyal subjects in Ireland. In what they termed the "Plantation of Ulster," the English under James I (who was also James VI of Scotland) began settling Scots in Ulster (Northern Ireland). The Scottish settlers were Presbyterian, and sometimes called "Protestant Irish" to distinguish them from the native Catholic Irish. Land was taken from the Irish nobility and granted to Scottish or English nobles. Families

31 Philip Rice and John Dahl. *Hunting Dogs.*

from lowland Scotland moved in to rent farms from the nobles. By 1690, one hundred thousand Scots had immigrated to Ulster.

The English government had settled Scots in Ireland because of their loyalty, but in less than a hundred years, the English managed to extinguish the Scots' loyalty and create much resentment. In 1662, the English government promulgated the Uniformity Act, which declared the Church of England (Anglican) the established church, it required Anglican ordination for all clergy, and promoted the Anglican Book of Common Prayer. Presbyterian marriages were not recognized by the state. Obviously, this did not set well with the Presbyterian Scots.[32] These and other laws intended to elevate Anglicanism over Presbyterianism created a lot of resentment.

Besides religious problems, the English insisted on creating economic problems for the Scottish settlers. In 1688, laws were passed restricting exports of woolen goods and linens from Ireland to England.[33] In the early eighteenth century, even the Northern Irish fishing industry was hampered by unnecessary regulation.[34]

All of these measures caused many Ulster Scots to migrate to England's American colonies. At first there was only a trickle of emigration, but by 1717, it turned into a flood. By 1776, two hundred fifty thousand Scotch-Irish had come to the colonies.[35] By 1776, between ten and twenty percent of the colonial population was Scotch-Irish. The English government may have repented their previous mistreatment when the Scotch-Irish provided fully twenty-five percent of

---

32 Donnelly, Colm J.

33 Patrick Kelly

34 *The Economist.* March 30, 2019.

35 Richard B. Drake. *A History of Appalachia.*

the soldiers in the Revolutionary armies. A Hessian captain is quoted as saying, "Call this war by whatever name you may, only, call it not an American Rebellion; it is nothing more or less than a Scotch-Irish Presbyterian Rebellion."[36]

The cur probably got this name from the Scotch-Irish, who spoke an archaic form of English. (They put the twang in country music; the Swiss added the yodel.) "Cur-dogge" was a Middle English word for a worthless mongrel. To the Scotch-Irish, unfamiliar with the boar dog, he looked like a worthless mongrel. When the Scotch-Irish learned the abilities of this "cur-dogge," they came to value him as much as their German neighbors did.

To both the Scotch-Irish and the German-speaking settlers, land was security. They were yeoman farmers, raising food primarily for the family's consumption. A number of vegetables were grown, but the major crop was corn. Corn was eaten as a vegetable, made into corn bread, fed to animals, and made into whiskey. George Vincent, who traveled among Scotch-Irish farmers in the nineteenth century, remarked that the farmer's diets consisted of "hogs and hominy."[37]

If there was a cash crop, it consisted of livestock. Frontier farmers raised cattle but mostly hogs. With the help of curs, the settlers drove livestock, sometimes over a hundred miles, to market. At stops along the route, were hog pens, where the hogs were kept when drives stopped for the night. Today there are dozens of "Hogpen" place names in the South. A cursory search of the internet shows thirty-eight geographical features named "Hogpen" or "Hog Pen." Most common is "Hogpen Branch." (A branch is a small stream.) There are also Hogpen Lakes, Creeks and Runs. In the Appala-

36 Jim Webb. *Born Fighting.* Broadway Books.

37 George Vincent. *Agriculture.* https:databases.lib.utk.edu.

chians, near the French Broad River, scene of the hog drives described in chapter 2, there are a number of "Hogpens." There is Hogpen Gap in North Carolina, Hogpen Hollow in Tennessee, and Hogpen Mountain in Virginia. By far the most interesting is the Hogpen Bar and Grill in Niota, Tennessee, where locals gather on Wednesday evenings to watch "oil wrestling." The number of Hogpen place names, and the fact that they're distributed throughout the South, is indicative of the importance of pork in pioneer diets and the importance of the dog that facilitated the gathering and driving of the hogs.

Most of the immigrants couldn't afford to buy farms in the settled areas of the colonies, but on the frontier land was available, sometimes given by colonial governments to advance settlement. It didn't matter that the natives might resist, the Scotch-Irish relished a good fight.

The Scotch-Irish were the predominant ethnic group on the frontier, but there was a considerable number of Germans. Sometimes there was friction between the two groups. "The Scotch-Irish had a reputation for impulsiveness, and were very politically active. The Germans, on the other hand, were sober and perhaps the best farmers in America."[38] Despite their differences, they were all farmers and they all hunted. One of the elements that brought them together was their dogs. The Scotch-Irish had scent hounds, which could trail and find game. Bear were hunted for food (especially for lard) and because they competed with, and sometimes killed, the settlers' open-range hogs. Scent hounds could find a bear but not keep him from running. The curs of the Germans were not as good as a scent hound at trailing a bear, but it could detain one until the hunters caught up.

---

38 Richard B. Drake. *A History of Appalachia.*

The pioneers learned to combine the talents of their dogs and hunt bear with "hounds and curs."[39] Sometimes the hounds and curs pursued the bear together, in the same pack, as in Faulkner's *The Bear* (chapter 2). At other times the curs were held on leash until the hounds had found the bear, then the curs would be freed to bite and keep the bear from running farther. Dogs helped meld these two peoples together. Descendants of Salzburgers and Dunkers joined with descendants of British (mostly Scotch-Irish) colonists to hunt, and to settle a continent. *De Bow's Review*, a magazine published in New Orleans, described a bear hunt using hounds and curs. The hunt took place on Sicily Island, Catahoula Parish, in 1851.

The boar dog had become a cur. A modern English dictionary defines "cur" as "a mongrel of low degree; a worthless dog." But in colonial America, and later on the frontier, a cur was certainly not worthless, and he was not a mongrel. A cur was a certain kind of dog, one very useful to people who had to survive in the American wilderness. The boar dog, the Catahoula, and any other dog that couldn't follow a scent trail worth a damn—but was hell on a bear or wild boar when it found one—was a cur.

After independence, the United States government encouraged westward movement and built some roads to facilitate it. In Georgia, at the southern end of the Appalachians, the federal government built the Federal Road from the Chattachooche River near Atlanta, northwest to Nashville. Why northwest? If the U.S. government wanted to encourage westward expansion, why not build the Federal Road due west, through Alabama? I believe the answer lies in the power of the Creek tribe.

---

39 Alfred R. Kilpatrick. "Early Life in the Southwest—The Bowies" *De Bow's Review.*

Most of Alabama was under Creek control until 1814, when Andrew Jackson defeated them in the Battle of Horseshoe Bend. Even after Jackson's victory, the Creeks defended their lands from white settlers until their forced removal to Oklahoma in the 1830s. Before then, most pioneers skirted Creek territory by taking the Federal Road to Nashville, then either turning westward or southwestward via the Natchez Trace. The Trace was a very old route, having been used by Native Americans for centuries before any white man ever set eyes on it. It led from Nashville to Natchez, on the Mississippi River.

Around the beginning of the nineteenth century, the number of settlers moving southwest along the Natchez Trace increased.[40] Louisiana did not become American until 1803, but the number of Americans moving down the Trace began to increase before then, because Spain had relinquished claim to most of what is now Mississippi and Alabama. Before the Treaty of San Lorenzo (1795), Spain claimed a line drawn due east of the mouth of the Yazoo River (present site of Vicksburg) as the northern boundary of their colony of West Florida. (Map 4.1) Spain had maintained a governor and a garrison at Natchez. In the Treaty of San Lorenzo, Spain and the United States agreed to regard the thirty-first parallel as the boundary. The Creeks still controlled most of Alabama, but this treaty opened most of Mississippi to American settlement. This may explain why Mississippi was settled and admitted to the union before Alabama. After the purchase of Louisiana, President Thomas Jefferson, realizing that the Natchez Trace was the key to settlement of the Mississippi Territory and the southern part of the Louisiana Purchase, ordered the U.S. Army to improve the Trace. Army engineers widened the road, built bridges, and drained swampy places. By 1809, the entire Trace was navigable by wagon.

40 Encyclopedia of Alabama

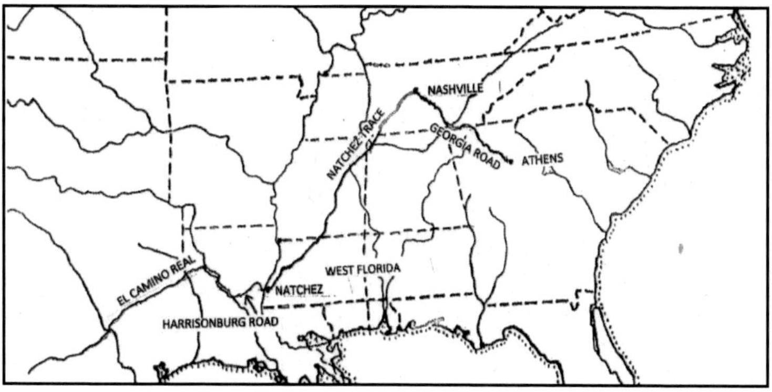

Map 4.1

In 1795, by the Treaty of San Lorenzo, Spain ceded all of West Florida north of the thirty-first parallel to the United States and pulled its soldiers out of Natchez. Eight years later, in 1803, the United States bought Louisiana.

Land available for settlement spurred migration westward. Settlers from Georgia, along with their curs, traveled the National Road (1) to Nashville, the Natchez Trace (2), and some crossed the Mississippi River and traveled the Harrisonburg Road and El Camino Real (3) into Louisiana and Texas. Their curs, important providers of food and safety, accompanied the pioneers.

The Louisiana Purchase spurred westward migration. Among the many families leaving Georgia for Louisiana was that of Jim Bowie, famous frontiersman and defender of the Alamo. The Bowie family traveled the Federal Road to the Nashville area and settled for a time, north of Nashville, across the Kentucky line. This is where Jim was born. After a few years in Kentucky, the Bowies followed the Natchez Trace to Natchez, crossed the Mississippi to Louisiana, and settled on Sicily Island, in Catahoula Parish. The Bowies owned curs, and legend has it that Jim and his brother Rezin, slept with a cur at their feet every night. Many American pioneers followed this route. Not all entered Louisiana. Some stopped on the way and made homes in Tennessee or Mississippi. Others continued to Texas.

Natchez is on a high bluff. (Fig. 4.1) Those who made it to Natchez stood on the bluff and marveled at the great river and miles and miles of forest beyond it. Some fifty years later, Frederick Law Olmsted, famous as the designer of Central Park in New York and of the Biltmore Estate in North Carolina, stood on this bluff. Olmsted: "I found myself … on the very edge of a stupendous cliff, and before me, an indescribable vast expanse of forest, extending on every hand to a hazy horizon."[41] Before the pioneers now, beyond the great river, was a lowland laced with myriad rivers and bayous. Geographically, it's a flood plain, not a delta, but they called it a delta, and the educated among them compared it to the Nile Delta of ancient Egypt. To reinforce the comparison, they chose place names from ancient Egypt. Cairo, Illinois was at the head of the delta. Farther downstream Memphis, Tennessee and Mansura, Louisiana were named after Egyptian places. Alexandria, Louisiana would fit right in, but it was named for a city father.

North of Vicksburg, and on the Mississippi side of the river, is the "Mississippi Delta," where the blues were born. Not far downstream, on the Louisiana side of the river, is the similar, but less famous, Louisiana Delta. Lower land in this giant flood plain was too swampy for agriculture. The higher land, especially the natural levees of the Mississippi was dry enough, although, when the Mississippi was unusually high, even the higher land could flood. Wealthy Americans would clear parts of the forest on the Louisiana side for plantations, but they chose to live on the high, dry, and less mosquito-ridden Mississippi side.

41 Frederick Law Olmsted

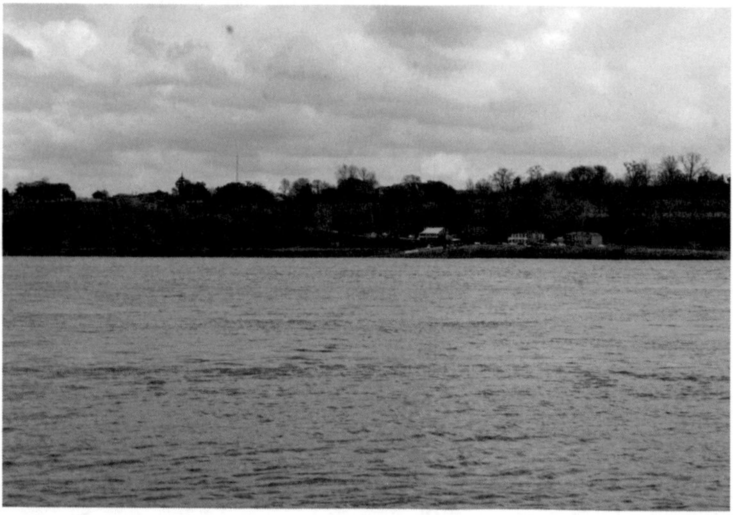

Fig. 4.1 The bluff at Natchez. Photo taken from the Louisiana side of the Mississippi River. The buildings at the base of the bluff (an area called "Natchez-under-the-hill) are at least two stories.

The pioneers had lived in uplands, but bottomlands, flood plains of rivers, were not entirely unfamiliar. The many rivers in the southeastern United States have flood plains, but these are tiny compared to that of the Mississippi. Many of the pioneers had farmed bottomlands; that was where the soil was most fertile, but when the water rose, they moved to the adjacent upland. The flood plain of the Mississippi is bordered on the east and west by bluffs. Natchez is on the bluff on the east. Sicily Island is high land on the west. It's called an island because it's surrounded by flood plain, and during high water, could be surrounded by water. From Natchez to Sicily Island is one of the narrower parts of the flood plain, and most of the settlers chose to cross the lowland, building homes on its western edge.

There are some natural levees in the flood plain, having been created by the smaller rivers (the Ouachita, Black,

Little). A wagon road through the flood plain used some of these higher places. The Ouachita River brushed against the west side of the flood plain at a place called Pine Point. The road ran from Vidalia, directly across the Mississippi from Natchez, to Sicily Island, then to Pine Point. At Pine Point, a ferry crossed the Ouachita River and some settlers built homes near the ferry landing. Their settlement was called Harrisonburg and the road became known as the Harrisonburg Road (formerly the Texas Road). It extended from Vidalia, through Harrisonburg, to the Red River near Alexandria. The Spanish had built a road, El Camino Real, from Mexico, through Texas, to Natchitoches, Louisiana, also on the Red River. The Natchez Trace, the Harrisonburg Road, and El Camino Real, provided a route used by many American pioneers to settle western Louisiana and Texas.

Most of the settlers chose to live on the uplands bordering the flood plain, but to their hogs, the flood plain was paradise. There is much more food for hogs in the hardwood forests of the flood plain than in the piney woods which covered the uplands. Hardwood forests produce hickory nuts, wild persimmons, muscadines, blackberries, other fruit, and a lot of one of the hog's favorites, acorns. Hogs grew numerous in the delta, especially as the number of bears was reduced.

The Catahoula Lake area supported an especially dense population of hogs. Catahoula Lake experiences major seasonal fluctuations in water level. In spring, when the Mississippi is high, water backs up in the Red, Black, Ouachita and Little rivers and into Catahoula Lake. As the water level recedes through the summer and fall, vast areas of the lake bottom are exposed. The large shallow lake almost dries out. The exposed lakebed is perfect habitat for the chufa plant. Late summer through fall, hundreds of hogs can be seen tearing up the lake bed rooting for nutritious chufa tubers.

The situation of the early settlers near Catahoula Lake was particularly fortuitous. The Lake lies near the western end of the flood plain. The settlers could live on and farm the higher land, while their hogs had excellent forage on the flood plain and the seasonally dry lake bed. In spring, when the Mississippi started to rise, the settlers built hog pens near the streams. When much of the flood plain was under water, the hogs were concentrated on higher ground, the natural levees of the rivers and bayous that drain the delta. Curs were now used to fill the pens with hogs. Some hogs were slaughtered, and unmarked pigs were ear marked. Not long after the village of Harrisonburg was founded, the men of the area began annual hog drives to Vidalia and Natchez. The Catahoula cur found the hogs in the forest, led them into pens, and drove them all the way to Natchez! Did I mention that this dog was invaluable to the pioneers?

The heyday of the hog dog began after the Civil War with the regular shipping of open range hogs from hog pens near the Black and Ouachita rivers to the "abattoir" in New Orleans. "Abattoir" is a French word for slaughterhouse, but no one called it the slaughterhouse. It was always "the abattoir." The abattoir was in New Orleans until 1875, when the state legislature moved it (the city, not the abattoir). The legislature decided that slaughterhouses shouldn't be located in cities. The abattoir was on the New Orleans side of the boundary with St. Bernard Parish. The legislature simply moved the boundary of the city so that the abattoir was outside the city.[42]

Steamboat shipping and passenger traffic in the lower Mississippi became important in the eighteen-teens. The first steamboat into the Catahoula country was the James Monroe. In 1819, the *James Monroe* sailed up the Black and

42 Peter Rusck, acknowledged expert on the abattoir. Personal conversation with the author. August 2019.

Ouachita rivers to Fort Miro, Louisiana. The people of Fort Miro were so impressed by what they saw as a good sign for their future, that they changed the name of their settlement to Monroe.

Settlers in the Catahoula country found it much easier to ship hogs by steamboat than to drive them to Natchez. There was no refrigeration, so hogs were transported live on the boats. They were confined on the rear deck, and passengers hated times when the wind blew from that direction.

In 1929, Roark Bradford, a writer and night city editor for *The Times-Picayune*, sailed on a steamboat from New Orleans to near Monroe. He took notes about the curs and hog pens when the steamboat stopped to load hogs. Bradford was amazed by the method of loading hogs:

> With the development of the breed of range hogs has come a breed of range dogs, or hog dogs, that is peculiar to that section. And further, a technic (sic) of hog handling that probably isn't duplicated anywhere in the world.
>
> Three men lift the hog over the pen and upon the shoulder of a waiting roustabout. The rouster who is to tote the hog on board receives him carefully, belly up and head pointing toward the rear. He gets a hand hold on each flank, and pulls down, to balance the weight of the hog, most of which is hanging over back of his shoulder. In this position, the hog is helpless. The weight of his whole body is resting on one spot on his backbone, and he cannot even wiggle or squirm.[43]

The most unusual cargo taken aboard the steamboats was pine knots. Resinous pine knots caught fire easily and were

43 Roark Bradford

used to start the fires in the steamboat boilers. The flood plain produced a lot of good hardwood, but no pine knots. Uplands near the western side of Catahoula Lake were covered with piney woods. Steamboats steamed up the Little River and into Catahoula Lake. In the 1840s and 50s, the steamboats *Rock River*, *Hannibal*, *Art*, and *Ellen* plied the lake, buying pine knots that settlers had gathered, hauled, and piled on the shore. The settlers took this opportunity to sell vegetables, pine knots, and hogs from pens that Catahoula curs had helped fill.

Bradford travelled through the Catahoula country in 1929. He describes Catahoulas, hogs, hog pens, the whole cultural complex, yet he never calls the dogs Catahoulas. They are always curs or hog dogs. The dogs have been here since around 1800, but I haven't found any reference to *Catahoula* curs that predates 1950. Don Abney, a respected Catahoula breeder and writer, has written: "the Catahoula is not mentioned specifically in the history books."[44] I don't think that's true. It just doesn't call him the Catahoula until sometime between 1930 and 1950.

How important was the cur to the Southern pioneer? The Loughmillers quote an elderly Big Thicket resident speaking of a typical pioneer:

> Although he used all kinds of dogs for one purpose or another, the cur was closest to his heart. It's the one dog the people of the thicket could not have done without. [The cur was used] every day for everything. A man used his cur to pen cattle … pen hogs … to protect him at night, and to hunt. He was used for hogs, bear, deer, cattle, panther, everything.[45]

44 Don Abney

45 Campbell and Lynn Loughmiller. *The Big Thicket Legacy.*

CHAPTER FIVE
REMNANTS OF THE FRONTIER: RELICT POPULATIONS OF CURS

In the last chapter, I chronicled the introduction of the German boar dog, ancestor of the cur, into the American colonies by German-speaking immigrants. Scotch-Irish neighbors of these German-speakers learned of the usefulness of the boar dog, or cur-dogge as the Scotch-Irish called them, and learned to use them. These people, Scotch-Irish, German, and some English were the pioneers who pushed the frontier from the coastal colonies, through the South and into Texas. They carried their culture, their way of life with them. There are backwater places in the South where pioneer ways held on into modern times. In these places, curs continued to be used in the old ways, especially to hunt or pen hogs. These out-of-the-way places became refugia for the curs that lived there. A refugium is a place where some kind of plant or animal survived when it disappeared from the rest of its range. An example is the Mongolian steppe where, in 1881, Col. Nicolai Przewalski encountered the species of wild horse that would later be named for him. The cur breeds that inhabited these refugia were named after places, physical characteristics, or the families who bred them. If there were no historical record of the pioneers' westward movement, it could still be traced through place names and breeds of cur left behind. One of these relict cur populations, the cracker cur, exists today in Georgia and Florida.

The English, both in England and in their North American colonies, referred to the Scotch-Irish as "crackers," an approximation of our word "braggart." As a letter written by a colonist to the Earl of Dartmouth explained: "I should explain to your Lordship what is meant by Crackers; a name they have got from being great boasters; they are a lawless set of rascals on the frontiers of Virginia, Maryland, the Carolinas, and Georgia, who often change their places of abode."[46] The quotation sums up commom perceptions of the Scotch-Irish. Their descendants in Georgia and Florida are sometimes called crackers even today. Curs owned and used by crackers became "cracker curs."

To my knowledge, the first record of the cur in Florida was made by William Bartram before the American Revolution. William Bartram's father was John Bartram, royal botanist to the English king. William's scientific interests reflected those of his father, but his political views probably did not because among William's friends were pro-independence Benjamin Franklin and Thomas Jefferson. Bartram became a noted botanist, naturalist, and ethnologist.

In 1774, Bartram explored Florida and befriended the Seminoles. He was an excellent illustrator, and did a sketch of Mico Chlucco, the "King of the Seminoles," as Bartram captioned his drawing. In his ponderously titled "Travels through North and South Carolina, Georgia, East and West Florida, the Cherokee Country, the Extensive Territories of the Muscogulges or Creek Confederacy, and the Country of the Choctaws," Bartram told of seeing curs among the Seminoles.[47]

In Seminole country were large populations of feral horses and cattle descended from those brought by the Spanish

46 James C. Clark
47 William Bartram

in the sixteenth century. Florida was a Spanish colony, and the Spanish shipped cattle to Cuba. The Seminoles became quite proficient cowboys. They tamed feral horses (later called "cracker ponies") and used their curs to roust cattle out of the scrub and swamps and drive them to ports on the Gulf of Mexico where the cattle could be sold for shipment to Cuba. Seminoles established ranches in the Gainesville area. Two Seminole chiefs important in the cattle trade, Chief Cowkeeper and Chief Billy Bowlegs, had very picturesque names. Chief Cowkeeper reportedly owned between seven thousand and ten thousand head of cattle. In 1774, Cowkeeper invited William Bartram to a feast and gave him permission to explore his tribal lands.

The United States obtained Florida from the Spanish in 1819. Because the Seminoles had been granting refuge to escaped African American slaves, war developed between the United States and the Seminoles. After the Second Seminole War (1835-42), the Seminoles were forced to leave their lands and travel to Oklahoma along what became known as the "Trail of Tears." White cracker cowboys took over the cattle business, and descendants of the curs William Bartram had seen among the Seminoles became cracker curs. During the Civil War, the Confederate government exempted cracker cowboys from the draft so that the Confederate Army could be supplied with beef.[48] This was especially true after the North took control of the Mississippi River, cutting off beef from Texas.

Cattle production in Florida was ended by the screwworm in the 1930s,[49] when ranchers brought cattle (possibly infected with screwworm larvae), from the Dust Bowl region of Oklahoma and Kansas. The screwworm fly deposited

48 Robert A. Taylor
49 M. E. Meadows

eggs in any wound in the hide of a cow The larvae entered the body of the animal and fed on it. Large numbers of screwworms could make beef unfit for consumption.

Today, the screwworm has been eradicated and there are again cattle in cracker country. Not the scrawny feral cattle but modern beef cattle. Some ranchers still use cracker curs, as do many hog hunters. The population of cracker curs (aka the Florida cur or Florida bulldog) is a remnant of what it used to be, and is considered a relict population.

As the frontier moved westward, several of these relict populations were left behind, and, today, attest to the movement of American pioneers and their dogs. For many families, the movement westward was not a uniform, continuous trek. Some families liked places along the way and decided not to go further. Not all of the stops were meant to be permanent. Sometimes, they stopped to allow a sick family member to recover without the constant jolting of a wagon. Sometimes, they needed to re-provision and stopped to raise a crop. Jim Bowie's family stopped near Nashville, just over the Kentucky line, later continuing to Louisiana. Jim was born during this Kentucky sojourn.[50] Whatever the reason, pioneer families occasionally stopped and, with their livestock, settled in places they favored.

As years went by, the world changed, but in a few backwaters, places time didn't touch, pioneers' descendants continued to live in the ways their ancestors had. They farmed, hunted, turned their livestock loose to feed in the woods, and used their curs to round them up. In the more modern places surrounding them, curs were no longer used and were replaced by more fashionable breeds. The places the pioneers stopped became refugia for old ways and traditional kinds of dogs.

50 Alfred R. Kilpatrick

One such refugium is in the southern Appalachians, from the Potomac through northern Georgia, where people still value their curs and refer to them as mountain curs. Some of the mountain people recognize the uniqueness of the cur and the contribution it's made to American history. They've organized the Original Mountain Cur Breeders' Association (OMCBA) to preserve the breed. This association, on its web site, recognizes the ancestry of the cur in dogs brought from Europe in colonial times. According to the breeders' association:

> It has been said by many old-timers, that without mountain curs … the southern mountains could not have been settled. When moving to a new home, pioneers provided for the mountain cur puppies. Baskets were slung across the backs of pack animals and the puppies rode. If no pack animals were available, family members carried the valuable puppies.

The OMCBA offers one reason for the relict breed's survival:

> Until World War II, the Mountain cur was still an asset to mountain people. Many a boy bought overalls and shoes, maybe coffee and sugar, with money from furs caught by mountain curs.

I especially like the following OMCBA quote:

> This dog is put down and ridiculed by some uninformed people because of the word 'cur.' In mountain cur, the word cur … has NO meaning of low or worthless.

Although the OMCBA recognizes the origin of their breed in dogs brought from Europe during the colonial era, curiously they also accept the common myth about the origin of the Catahoula cur. The OMCBA web site speaks of Hernando DeSoto bringing brindle curs when he explored the Mississippi River. The site states that "settlers found the brindles when they came south" 250 years later. The OMCBA must have gotten this information from Catahoula cur people, but, as discussed, there is no evidence that DeSoto's dogs were ancestral to the Catahoula. There are several cur breeds in the South, all of which share physical and behavioral characteristics. It seems logical that they also share their ancestry.

Near the end of the eighteenth century, pioneers began to move westward into Tennessee and the Mississippi Territory. By the Treaty of San Lorenzo (1796), Spain had ceded most of southern Mississippi and Alabama to the United States. Most of the pioneers traveled the Natchez Trace, a route Native Americans had used for centuries. The Trace extended 444 miles, from Nashville southwestward to Natchez on the Mississippi River. Even settlers from Georgia traveled to Nashville rather than due west through Alabama because the powerful Creek tribe controlled Alabama until 1814. In southwest Mississippi, at the southern end of the Trace is the black mouth cur.

When I first heard of them, from Charlie Davis, I had wondered whether they had black tongues, as the chow does, but it is their muzzle that is black. The black mouth cur is a yellow or red dog with a black muzzle, or "melanistic mask." The book *Old Yeller* was written about a black mouth cur, but a yellow labrador retriever mix was used in the 1957 movie. Black mouth curs come in yellow (or tan) and red. Almost all have the black muzzle.

Among the British immigrants to America in the eighteenth century, was the Ladner family. They eventually settled, with their curs, in southwest Mississippi. The Ladners, like the Plotts of Plott hound fame, used planned matings to improve their breed. Thanks to the family's extensive breeding records, L. H Ladner, in 1964, was able to secure recognition of the black mouth cur from the National Kennel Club. The National Kennel Club lists the dog as the "Ladner yellow black mouth cur."

To summarize the trail so far: in Georgia and Florida, the cracker cur is a descendant of the boar dog. In the southern Appalachians, near the beginning of the Natchez Trace, are the Plott hound and the mountain cur. At the southern end of the Natchez Trace is the black mouth cur.

The Catahoula cur is next along the trail of the pioneers. The Catahoula's refugium is at the end of the Natchez Trace, just across the Mississippi from Natchez and the black mouth cur.

The Catahoula Lake country is unique. The lake is in the floodplain, but northwest of the lake are piney uplands, which are safe from spring floods. Hogs love to root out pine seedlings, but they thrive on the various foods provided by the bottomland hardwood forests of the flood plain. These forests are rich in acorns, hickory nuts, blackberries, and other nutritious hog foods, but these are found in many places. What makes the Catahoula country unique is a large freshwater lake with a major annual fluctuation in water level. Low water exposes miles of lake bottom, allowing a grass-like plant, called chufa, to sprout. The chufa, or nut sedge, has nutritious nodules on its roots. At low water, hundreds of feral hogs can be seen spread over the lake bed rooting for chufa roots.

During the nineteenth and early twentieth centuries, steamboats loaded hogs, either at Catahoula Lake, or at Harrisonburg, for shipment to slaughterhouses. Steamboats traveling down the Black, Red, and Mississippi Rivers could deliver hogs to Baton Rouge, New Orleans, or the many river towns on the river. All of these factors allowed the Catahoula Lake area to become preeminent in using curs to herd and hunt hogs and gave the Catahoula cur, or Catahoula leopard, its name.

Following the pioneers westward, to southeast Texas, is an area of thick woods with copious undergrowth. A traveler wrote in 1895, "This day, passed through the thickest woods I ever saw. It surpasses any country for brush."[51] Known as the "Big Thicket," this is the refugium of what I'll call the "Thicket cur," although the people of the Thicket generally call him simply the "cur."

Campbell and Lynn Loughmiller are naturalists who roamed the Thicket, studying its creatures for nine years before publishing *The Big Thicket Legacy*. They had come to realize that the people of the Thicket, along with their dogs, were the most interesting element of the whole Thicket mosaic. Most of the people are direct descendants of the original settlers. They know the lifeways of the settlers (still follow many of them) and were excellent informants for the Loughmillers.

In 1917, Hardy Farmer, a west Texas rancher, moved his cattle to the Big Thicket to escape a drought. Farmer "couldn't understand why they valued a dog in the Thicket more than they valued a horse on the range. Dogs! No place on earth has as many dogs per person as the Thicket." The Loughmillers quote Big Thicket native Leak Bevil referring to a Big Thicket pioneer:

51 Campbell and Lynn Loughmiller

> Although he used all kinds of dogs for one purpose or another, the cur was closest to his heart. It is the one dog the people of the Thicket [and southern pioneers in general] could not have done without.[52]

Most Thicket curs are various shades of yellow to brown, and some have the melanistic mask of Mississippi's black mouth cur. Some are brindle or black. Although many Thicket settlers passed through Catahoula country on their way to the Thicket, the area's curs don't include leopards.

In the nineteenth century, there were hog drives from the Thicket to Beaumont, TX. It took two days to cover forty-five miles. One cur was all it took once the hogs got started, although there were often three on the drive. The Thicket is one of three places where I've found reports of hog drives, the first being along the French Broad River, as recounted in chapter 3. The second was from Harrisonburg, in Catahoula Parish, Louisiana, to Natchez, Mississippi. It would be interesting to know whether the "yuh yuh yuh" command was used in the Big Thicket and Catahoula Parish as it was on the French Broad. [53]

West of the Big Thicket, the cedar-covered hills of central Texas, where the southern frontier became the western frontier, provided another refugium for a cur. In 1858, the Lacy family traveled to Texas in a covered wagon. They brought their curs, an important part of their livelihood, with them. Like the many pioneer families who preserved their family lines of curs, the Lacy family valued and preserved their strain. Today, the Texas blue lacy is the state dog of Texas.

52 Ibid

53 Eliot Wigginton

According to the National Lacy Dog Association, "Lacies come in three colors, red, blue and tri." (Blue means gray. This is true among mountain people, Catahoula people, and now Lacy fanciers. Similarly, a blue tic hound has gray tics, or spots, in white portions of his coat.) The dogs referred to as tri-colored by Lacy fanciers are black-and-tan along with some other color. Curs are not typically black-and-tan (though there are black-and-tan Catahoulas), but there are black-and-tan scent hounds.

Like Catahoulas and cracker curs, lacies have been known by a few different names, including "Texas blur lacy." The National Lacy Dog Association gets quite perturbed about this: The association insists that the breeds "correct name is lacy dog or lacy hog dog, not Texas blue lacy." The man responsible for adding "blue" was probably H.C. Wilkes, one of a few breeders who kept the breed alive when it went through a period of low population. Wilkes started calling his dogs "blue lacies" (probably because they were gray). In 2001, the Texas legislature named the lacy their state dog, and he became the "Texas blue lacy."

Tom Stodghill, founder of the Animal Research Foundation, the first organization to register both the Catahoula and the Texas blue lacy, was quoted in 1976: "The style of work of the Texas lacy cowdog is identical to that of the Catahoula leopard."[54] Tom could have added, "and all other curs."

As the frontier moved westward, it left records, not just in writing, but also in flesh and blood. We've found relict breeds of curs along the route of the pioneers, from Georgia and Florida (cracker cur) and the southern Appalachians (mountain cur) to Nashville, down the Natchez Trace (black mouth cur), across the Mississippi to Catahoula Lake (Cata-

54 Tom Stodghill

houla cur) to eastern Texas (Thicket cur) westward to central Texas (blue lacy).

The colonization of the American west was realized by both the pioneers and their dogs, especially the cur.

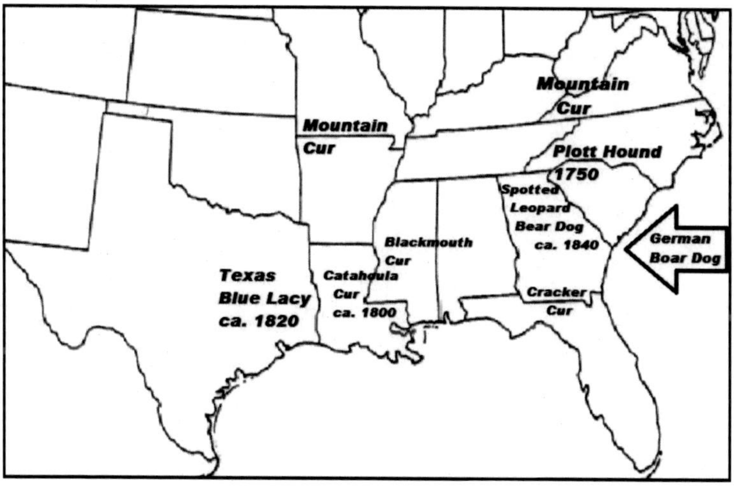

Map 5.1 Descendants of the German boar dog and distribution of cur breeds. Map by Don Shannon.

All of these cur breeds are descended from German boar dogs brought to the British Colonies on the east coast before the American Revolution. The cur accompanied the frontiersmen as they settled the South, and they were instrumental in feeding and protecting pioneer families.

CHAPTER SIX
DECLINE OF THE OPEN RANGE

In order for the cur to become as vital to the Southern frontier as he was, several elements were necessary. Obviously curs and hogs were necessary, so is good hog habitat, but there is one more essential element: the practice of "open range." To colonists the whole world was pasture. Livestock could be turned loose to find their own food. In this way, the abundant resources of the forest could be converted to farm income. This practice, called open range, was used for hogs, cattle, sometimes horses, and in the daytime, chickens. Curs are most useful where there is open range, because they surpass other breeds at hunting and penning woods hogs. Dogs of many breeds can be used to herd cattle, but only the cur is called a hog dog!

Open range is necessary for the harvesting of free-ranging hogs to be profitable, and finding and penning free-roaming hogs is the cur's specialty. Where open range is outlawed, as it is in increasingly more of the South,[55] no one can legally own feral hogs, ear-marked or not. As long as there are hogs loose in the woods, the cur will have a role to play, but when open range is no longer practiced, and hog populations are eliminated by land clearing for agriculture or development, the cur loses much of his usefulness. Open range was a successful method of stock raising as long as there was enough

55 J. Crawford King, "The Closing of the Southern Range: An Exploratory Study" *The Journal of Southern History 48(1):53-70. 1982.*

wilderness, that is, as long as population density was low and farms were far apart.

With time, population increased and more land was cleared for farming. The wilderness was smaller, but the herds of livestock were larger, because after all, the stock owner had no incentive to limit his herds, he wasn't paying for their feed. Hogs set out to feed in the shrinking, now overcrowded wilderness, couldn't resist fields of corn, beans, peas, etc. Owners of woods hogs benefited from open range, but farmers had a problem keeping hogs out of their crops.

As far back as 1785, there were complaints about the practice of open range (at that time in South Carolina). In the nineteenth century, the "Farmer's Register, a prominent agricultural journal of the time, led the fight against open range. A planter wrote a letter to the editor stating: "It is notorious that those [who] have the most stock have the least land to graze." Planters complained that because of hogs they didn't own, they were forced to over-invest in "fencing, buckshot, and lawyer's fees."[56]

The evolution of laws dealing with open range is engaging. When problems between planters and open-range hog raisers first arose in the American colonies, colonial governments, and later state governments, tended to take the side of the animal owner, not the side of the planter whose crop was being devoured. As early as 1632 in Virginia, a law required farmers to fence crops "or else to plant upon theire owne peril." In Georgia, if a farmer failed to fence his crops, any "trespass or damage so ever he shall receive or sustain by hogs, cattle, or horses shall be at his own loss."[57]

In time every Southern state, in order to minimize disputes, described a "legal fence," which must enclose plant-

56 Ibid.

57 Ibid.

ed fields. These laws specified the height of the fence and the distance between rails. If a farmer did not have a legal fence and he shot an animal devouring his crop, he could be held liable for triple the value of the animal. Horace Greeley, respected nineteenth-century journalist, wrote that "Excessive fencing is peculiarly an American abuse, which urgently cries out for reform."[58] Greeley was clearly on the side of the farmer.

The Civil War also affected the open range debate. The war destroyed many fences, and took into the Confederate Army many of the men who may have fixed them. The abolition of slavery made some stockmen more amenable to outlawing the practice of open range because the hungry freedmen were killing pigs. Farmer James Clanton complained in the Register: "We cannot raise a turkey, chicken, or hog in consequence of stealing by negroes … We dare not turn stock out at all."[59]

The open range debate became one of "haves" versus "have-nots." J. Crawford King, in an article published in the journal *Southern History*, relates an 1880 statement of one John Henry Dent, a prosperous planter: "All the negroes and whites who own no land, and by right and justice should … not vote … will vote for fencing [of crops, not animals.]"[60] Dent wanted the animals fenced in.

Even some stock raisers objected to open range. Those desirous of improving their stock were concerned that their hogs of new and improved breeds may mate with grubby open range animals. Open range hogs were lean animals called "razorbacks" or "woods alligators" with their visible backbones, and long snouts. Sam Hilliard, an LSU geogra-

58 Shawn E. Kantor

59 Ibid

60 J. Crawford King, ibid.

pher, described the typical open range hog in *Hog Meat and Hoe Cake: Food Supply in the Old South 1840-1860*:

> The practice of allowing, indeed encouraging, swine to forage for much of their food led to a 'natural selection' that placed a premium on fleetness of foot, hardiness, wariness, in short, on the techniques of survival in the forest. Ultimately, these attributes of the semi-feral animals were not conducive to rapid gains in flesh. The southern razorback hog was almost universally maligned as being more like a greyhound than like a pig.[61]

Jess Rickman, from *Foxfire 3*, echoes Hilliard: "Hogs were smaller and had a nose about three times as long as the tame ones do now. We called 'em jug drinkers." The stockman trying to improve pork production would not likely want his prize sows mating with range hogs.[62]

Open range became less popular after the Civil War for all the reasons mentioned, but also for aesthetic reasons. In 1880, the town council of Milledgeville, Georgia, received this complaint (one of my favorite quotes) from a group of ladies who objected to goat poop on their porches:

> a large group of goats promenade the streets by night and take lodging on our porches, which in the morning present … a filthy and disgusting appearance. We cannot look upon it with Christian resignation.[63]

61 Sam Hilliard. "Pork in the Ante-Bellum South: The Geography of Self-Sufficiency" *Annals, Association of American Geographers 53(9)*. September 1969.

62 Eliot Wigginton. *Foxfire 3*. New York: Knopf Doubleday Publishing Group. 1975.

63 J. Crawford King, ibid.

Railroads also campaigned against open range. They were held liable for injuries to animals hit by trains. The railroads complained that some unscrupulous stock owners "salted" the tracks (put blocks of salt on the tracks) in hopes of attracting their animals and having them hit by a train. William Faulkner reminisced about "the old halcyon days when even the [railroad] companies considered their southern branches ... the legitimate prey of all who dwelt beside them."[64]

Early in the twentieth century, as the number of automobiles gradually increased, motorists added their voices to those clamoring for an end to open range. Too often, roads were blocked or motorists were hurt in collisions with cattle or hogs.[65]

Even timber companies opposed open range. After cutting the South's longleaf pine forests, they were forced to replant. Unfortunately, open range hogs were rooting up their seedlings as fast as they could be planted. Laurence Walker, forestry professor and expert on southern forests, explains that the food reserves of a longleaf seedling are "stored mainly as starch in the thickened taproot and are as nutritious as a parsnip." Turpentine is a product of pine, and Walker jokes that a razorback hog eats so many pine seedlings, that, when cooked down, will yield "a pound of lard and a gallon of turpentine."[66]

Free-ranging hogs have been linked to soil erosion. Hogs rooting for grubs and roots loosened the soil and made it more susceptible to being washed away. A common theme of environmental writers is "the tragedy of the commons." In eighteenth century England, many villages had some

64 Ibid.

65 Ibid.

66 Laurence C. Walker. *Forests: A Naturalist's Guide to Woodland Trees. Austin: University of Texas Press.* 1990.

land held in common, where any villager could graze his animals. The commons belonged to everyone in general, but to no one in particular, so no one in particular took care of them. Overgrazing removed vegetation, which held the soil in place, and the commons became the most eroded land in the vicinity of the village.[67] The commons were overgrazed, never fertilized, and resulting erosion never checked. In parts of Louisiana today, hogs are damaging levees with their rooting. Where woods hog populations are dense, there is a "tragedy of the commons" all over again.

In Louisiana, as time passed, plantations spread along the Mississippi and Red Rivers. Cities and towns grew. Large scale agriculture cleared more and more land, especially for cotton and soybeans. Timber companies and paper companies replanted forests. All of these activities were incompatible with open range. Consequently, the legislature gradually restricted the practice, which was finally eliminated in Louisiana in November, 2001.[68] LaSalle Parish, site of Catahoula Lake, was the last parish with legal open range.

Where, then, does that leave the Catahoula cur? He is most useful when hogs are allowed to run free. The one thing at which curs surpass all other breeds is catching free ranging hogs. If his specialty is taken away from him, will the Catahoula survive? Will this breed so instrumental in the settling of the South become extinct? The Southern frontier cannot be completely understood without a knowledge of the contribution of this dog.

---

67 Garrett Hardin

68 Louisiana Revised Statute 3:2891 *Swine Prohibited from Running at Large.* https://www.lawserver.com/law/state/louisiana/la-laws/louisiana_revised_statutes

Several people in the Catahoula Lake area, some of them descendants of those who brought the Catahoula to Louisiana, recognized this problem and in 2012 formed the Working Catahoula Association (WCA). Even if Catahoulas survived as pets, watch dogs, or even cattle dogs, if they lost their one unique characteristic, the ability to catch free ranging hogs, they would not be the same kind of dog that helped settle the South. Members of the WCA foresaw the deterioration of the "work ethic" of the Catahoula. By work ethic, the WCA refers to the dog's ability to do the work Catahoulas have traditionally done. They saw the need to preserve, within the breed, the work ethic, the same qualities which had made the Catahoula so important to the pioneers. Members of the WCA also knew how important open range was to the development of the Catahoula:

> What actually helped develop the breed was the method by which the early settlers ranched. All lands in Louisiana were open range, livestock was allowed to free range with no fencing or barriers.

As Louisiana's population and economy grew, with some of her people switching to more profitable occupations, laws limited open range. Open range was ended in LaSalle Parish in November, 2001. As the WCA summarizes:

> With that single drastic change [outlawing open range], a way of life that had supported many families for generations was gone, along with that, the need for the working Catahoula. Some of the descendants of those who had developed the breed saw the need, not to just

preserve, but to preserve the breed by work ethic, the same qualities that were an integral part of its history.[69]

Open range was an important factor in making the Catahoula what he is. Without open range, how will the Catahoula change? When there is no longer a need to find a hog in the woods and hold it by the ears, will Catahoulas lose the ability to do this? When there is no longer a necessity to lead a herd of woods hogs into a pen, will Catahoulas, still be able to do this?

The WCA holds competitions in cattle herding, scent trailing, treeing climbing animals, and baying hogs. To my knowledge, there are no competitions involving finding and holding feral hogs and leading hogs into hog pens, so despite the best efforts of the WCA, the Catahoula cur may become a changed breed.

69 Working Catahoula Association. "History of the WCA," *Working Catahoula Association.* Copyright 2019 Accessed May 2017. https://workingcatahoulaassociation.com/history-of-the-wca/

CHAPTER SEVEN
THE CATAHOULA TODAY

In the preceding chapter, I argued that open range was instrumental in shaping the Catahoula cur. Now open range has ended. What does that portend for the future of Louisiana's state dog? The Catahoula, and curs in general, are no longer indispensable as they were on the frontier, but a dog who wasn't intelligent and adaptable could never have survived the frontier. Pioneers didn't keep dogs that couldn't pay their way. They couldn't afford to. "That dog don't hunt" was often a death sentence.

In Louisiana, there are still people who use Catahoulas to capture and ear-mark the pigs born to their open-range sows in the woods and swamps, though the ear marks are no longer legally protected. A number of rural Louisiana back yards continue to boast large scalding kettles, into which the field-dressed carcass of a hog can be lowered, but because most of the men now commute to jobs, hog hunting is now more of a weekend diversion (when there's no football game on TV).

One still widespread use for Catahoulas is herding. Cattlemen still use dogs to herd cattle, especially in wooded or bushy country, where many cattle might otherwise be overlooked. One rancher described his Catahoula as a "four-footed cowpoke."

Many owners I've spoken to swear on the Catahoula's value as a watchdog and protector. They're big enough and bold enough to make any intruder have second thoughts. Catahoulas become extremely bonded with their human families and are brave enough to put themselves between their families and any threat.

The Catahoula's merled coat and interesting glass eyes make him an increasingly popular pet and show dog. Becoming a show dog, in the opinion of some, wouldn't be an unalloyed good thing. It would certainly change the Catahoula. Geoffrey English, an authority on hunting dogs, has pointed out that "for better than half a century, the sporting dog breeds have gone in two directions. Field breeders are producing the athletes and show breeders are producing the models."[70] Charles Frisk, of Green Bay, Wisconsin, who hunts with bird dogs, noted this phenomenon in cocker spaniels: "I've always thought it a shame that the field bred cocker pretty much died out and was replaced by the long-coated show strains."[71] It's very possible that Catahoulas could meet a similar fate.

As we learned in chapter 3, hunting dogs inherit an aptitude for the work of their breed. Breeders who use dogs to hunt try to breed dogs that will perform well, whereas breeders of show dogs prioritize the physical characteristics called for in the breed's standard. The show dog world is different from the Catahoula's hardscrabble roots, and it may not be the future that organizations like the Working Catahoula Association have in mind.

Dog shows are conducted by the organizations that register dogs, and their shows usually include only breeds that the organization formally recognizes. The big boys among registering organizations are the United Kennel Club (UKC) and the American Kennel Club (AKC). When I finished my master's thesis in 1969, there were only three small organizations and one national group, the UKC, that were knowingly registering curs of any kind. I say "knowingly"

70 Geoffrey English
71 Charles Frisk

because the UKC had been registering Plott Hounds since 1946, but as scent hounds, not curs. In chapter 5 we discussed the two kinds of Plotts, and the apparent inclusion of scent hound ancestry in the long-eared Plott. The German boar dogs that Johannes Plott brought from Germany gave rise to America's curs, not to its scent hounds!

In 1995, the UKC, which as mentioned had long been registering Plott hounds, accepted the Catahoula under the name "Louisiana Catahoula leopard dog." Until 1998, neither of the big national organizations registered any cur breed under the cur name. I've been asked whether there was prejudice against the name "cur." I don't know, but there are a couple of more likely reasons, first that most of the cur breeds are known only within a small area, and second, that some of them (including the Catahoula) differ widely in physical characteristics. Even people who know Catahoulas sometimes can't tell whether a dog is a Catahoula. Their abilities, more than their physical characteristics, are what mark them as Catahoulas.

In 1998, the UKC went wild and accepted five cur breeds: the mountain cur, the Stephens cur, the treeing Tennessee brindle, the black mouth cur, and the treeing cur. Actually, three of the five are strains of the same breed. The Stephens cur has long been recognized as a strain of mountain cur bred by the Stephens family of southeastern Kentucky. The treeing Tennessee brindle was created in the 1960s by the Rev. Earl Phillips, from brindle mountain curs he collected from the Ozarks, the southern Appalachians, and points in between. The cur breeds recognized by the UKC are shown in Table 7.1.

DATE	BREED	GROUP	CUR OR SCENT HOUND
1946	Plott hound	Scent hound	Short-eared Plott is a cur. Long-eared Plott is part scent hound.
1995	Louisiana Catahoula leopard dog	Herding	Cur
1998	Mountain cur	Scent hound	Cur
1998	Stephens cur	Scent hound	Cur
1998	Treeing Tennessee brindle	Scent hound	Cur
1998	Black mouth cur	Scent hound	Cur

Table 7.1 Cur breeds accepted by the United Kennel Club.[72]

The UKC placed the Catahoula in its herding group, and the other six cur breeds in its scent hound group. There is some justification in the placing of the Plott hound in the scent hound group, because the long-eared Plott has some scent hound ancestry, but the others are all curs, who cannot follow a ground scent trail unless its fresh. Curs have hot noses! I wrote the UKC and asked them to explain this placement but got no response.

In the course of studying the Catahoula and other curs, I learned several differences between scent hounds and curs. The following short list may help keep them in mind:

72 Created by author from UKC data.

QUALITY	SCENT HOUND	CUR
Use in hunting	Trailing—Finding the quarry	Holding and delaying the quarry until arrival of the hunters
Trailing ability (nose)	Cold nose—Can follow a cold scent trail	Hot nose—Can follow only a hot, or fresh trail
Position of head while hunting	Nose to ground—searching for or following a scent trail	Head up, trying to catch a scent in the wind or sight the quarry
Voice	Drawl	Higher-pitched crop
Use of voice when trailing	Bays on trail	Silent until quarry is found
Length of ear	Long	Shorter than that of a hound

Table 7.2 Scent hound vs. cur characteristics.

The pioneers brought both hounds and curs westward with them. The pioneers knew the difference between the two and used the dogs in different roles when hunting, as they said, "with hounds and curs." The hounds with their cold noses were relied upon to find the quarry. Curs, with their perhaps foolhardy willingness to attack even a bear, were used to keep the bear or hog occupied while the hunters caught up.

The AKC, more conservative than the UKC, has fully accepted no cur breed. Instead, the AKC has instituted the Foundation Stock Service (FSS) to "allow purebred breeds to continue developing while enjoying the security of a reliable avenue to maintain their records." The five AKC curs and their dates of admission into the FSS are:

DATE	BREED	GROUP	CUR OR SCENT HOUND
1995	Treeing Tennessee brindle	Hound	Cur
1996	Catahoula leopard dog	Herding	Cur
2006	Plott hound	Hound	Short-eared Plott is a cur. Long-eared Plott is part scent hound.
2012	American leopard hound	Hound	Looks like a hound/ Catahoula cross*
2017	Mountain cur	Hound	Cur

Table 7.3. Cur breeds in the foundation stock service (AKC).[73]

*The American leopard hound looks like a Catahoula cur with a scent hound's ears.

The AKC doesn't have a scent hound group, as the UKC does. Instead, the AKC has a "hound" group and assigns scent hounds and sight hounds to it. Curs, and other dogs who hunt with their heads up (basenjis, greyhounds, Irish wolfhounds, etc) are called sight hounds, and can correctly be placed in the hound group.

Fortunately for the future of the breed, the Catahoula is a multi-talented animal. One excellent example of a multi-talented Catahoula is Ladyhawke, bred and trained by Don Abney of Abita Springs, Louisiana. Ladyhawke was certified as both a search and rescue dog and a narcotics detection dog. Don explains that in search and rescue work, a Catahoula has an advantage over a scent hound, because the hound will put his nose to the ground and follow a scent trail with all its twists and turns until he finds the lost person. In cases where time is important, i.e. a lost toddler, freezing weather, or a lost person who needs medication, a Catahoula will often find the person quicker than

73 Created by author from AKC data.

will a hound, because the Catahoula searches with his head up, trying to get a scent in the wind, or perhaps sight the lost person. His route will often be more direct than the hound's.

Seeing curs get more recognition, and even entering the dog show world, is encouraging. This helps to ensure that these dogs, which have been so important in Southern history, will not disappear.

AFTERWORD

Fifty-two years ago, I set out to study the Catahoula hog dog and discovered that it was a descendant of the German boar dog. Check the internet today, and you'll find that none of the "authorities" agree with me. Most who write about the Catahoula's origin repeat the DeSoto myth.

Judging by dictionary definitions of "cur," curs are disdained, if not held in outright contempt. Yet of the nine states that designate state dogs, four have adopted descendants of the German boar dog, including three cur breeds. Pennsylvania adopted the Great Dane, which, like the curs, is a descendant of the boar dog. Louisiana, in 1979, proclaimed the Louisiana Catahoula leopard dog its state dog. North Carolina adopted the Plott hound in 1989, and in 2005 Texas named as its state dog the Texas blue lacy.[74]

Back at LSU, in 1970, I was defending my master's thesis. My work was being judged by a committee of three distinguished professors. They were Dr. Milton Newton, my major professor, Dr. W. G. Haag, a respected professor of anthropology in our Department of Geography and Anthropology, and Dr. Fred B. Kniffen, a well-respected scholar and one of the foremost geographers in the world. I knew from an earlier conversation with Dr. Kniffen that I would have to defend not only my scholarship, but the appropriateness of my topic. What does a dog have to do with geography?

---

74 State Symbols, Emblems & Icons. STATE Symbols USA. n.p n.d. Date accessed Oct 21, 2020. http://statesymbolsusa.org/us/symbols/state.

My answer was in two parts. First, I argued that cultural geographers study material culture and that domesticated animals are cultural artifacts in that they are developed by people. People decide which domesticated animals will pass their characteristics to the next generation. Nature would never have produced our breeds of dogs, cattle, hogs, or other domesticated animals. They would have been weeded out in any "survival of the fittest" test. Can you picture a Chihuahua running with a pack of wolves? Natural selection produces wild species. Artificial selection, that of the breeder, produces domesticated varieties.

Second, the Catahoula has been an important part of the human-land relationship in the Catahoula area. The Catahoula helped local people survivef in their environment. The relationship of a people to its environment, mediated by culture, is a revered tradition in geography. Dr. Kniffen, a cultural geographer himself, congratulated me on my answer.

A moment almost as satisfying as my thesis defense occurred a few years later. My wife and I were watching a television news broadcast about a diplomatic meeting involving President Gerald Ford and President Anwar Sadat of Egypt when something I saw on the screen almost made me fall out of my chair. The meeting took place at Schloss Klessheim palace in Salzburg, Austria. Salzburg is on the German border, the very homeland of the German boar dogs and the Salzburgers who brought boar dogs to Georgia. There on the wall behind the presidents was a mural depicting two merled German boar dogs, looking for all the world like Catahoulas. And what were they doing? Chasing a hog!

APPENDIX I
THE OTHER THREE

In earlier chapters we learned of four types of dog brought to what became the United States by early settlers. We learned of the boar dog, carried to North America from the mountainous areas where Germany, Austria, and Switzerland meet. The boar dog is the ancestor of the various cur breeds so important on the Southern frontier.

We also learned that British settlers, English and Scotch-Irish, brought with them three other types of dogs: small terriers called feists, to control vermin and act as watch dogs; collie-type shepherd dogs to help with cattle and sheep; and scent hounds to help in the hunt. We know the story of the boar dog, but what happened to the other three?

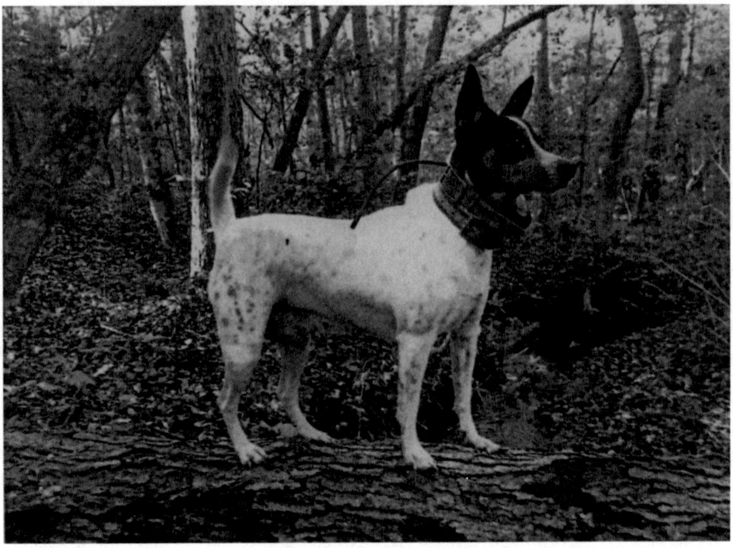

Fig. A1.1 Shadowtail's River Queen. A champion feist, ready for action. Image courtesy of Shadowtail Kennels.

THE FEIST

If the feist had died out, it would at least have left an adjective in our language. The American Heritage Dictionary defines the adjective "feisty" as "touchy, quarrelsome, or spirited." Maybe feists are touchy, maybe quarrelsome too, but they are definitely spirited. The Google Online Dictionary says a feist is "a small mixed-breed snappy, belligerent little dog." Judging from these definitions, feists are not highly regarded.

Feists do have some of the qualities attributed to them. They are small, about the size of a Jack Russell terrier or a Manchester terrier, and have erect ears. Occasionally they are born with only the nub of a tail. Feists are terriers, and terriers tend to be active and aggressive toward strangers.

The bravery of this little dog is illustrated by this story from frontier days. I don't know whether it's true, but having gotten to know a few feists myself, it could easily be:

A young pioneer woman was struggling to pacify her crying baby while hanging wet clothes on a line, which her husband had strung. To add to her problems, behind her, her feist was barking up a storm. She half-turned to yell at the dog, but the words never came as she froze in fear! Her feist was between her and a grown mountain lion! The young woman snatched up her baby and ran for the cabin door. Once safely inside, she sat on the floor with her back to the door until she could catch her breath and her heart stopped pounding.

The young woman anxiously related her experience when her husband returned from the hunt with his hounds and curs. He immediately set out with his dogs in search of the lion. The trail was fresh, and after a short search, they found the mountain lion snarling from a big oak. The man shot him. He set to work skinning the lion, and he found, in the lion's stomach, his brave little feist.[75]

Like the cur, the feist survived in isolated places, especially the southern Appalachians and the Ozarks. Also like the cur, the feist had a different appellation in every mountain holler. Some of these are the mountain feist, the smokey mountain feist, the old-timey mountain feist, the pencil-tail feist, and the snowball feist.

With the end of the frontier, the feist was still needed. The end of open range handicapped the cur, but not the feist. Rats and mice were a problem wherever there was food. Feists were kept around silos and wherever grain was shipped. Urban areas had rat problems that the feist helped solve until chemical pesticides largely replaced it in the mid-twentieth century.

---

75 Mark Derr

When Theodore Roosevelt was president, his feist-type dog, Skip (or Scamp) helped fight a serious rat infestation in the White House.[76] Roosevelt was credited with giving the breed the name "rat terrier," but in fact they'd carried that name since the 1890s when some were imported from Britain for use in the "sport" of rat baiting. Rat terriers were thrown into pits with several rats and the dog who killed the most rats in a given time period was the winner.[77]

There is now a shorter-legged version of the rat terrier called the Teddy Roosevelt terrier in honor of the president. The UKC granted recognition to the classic rat terrier and the type B rat terrier (the Teddy Roosevelt terrier) in 1999. The AKC recognized the rat terrier in 2013.[78] Whether called the rat terrier or the Teddy Roosevelt terrier, the dog is a feist, with all of the attributes of a feist.

The feist was an important part of the frontier, and he served on American farms throughout the nineteenth and most of the twentieth century. Today, feists are used to hunt squirrel and rabbit and often kept as pets or show dogs.

---

76 Bishop, Joseph Bucklin, ed. *Theodore Roosevelt's Letters to His Children*. New York: Charles Scribner's Sons, 1919.

77 See Henry Mayhew's 1850 account of the practice in *London Labour and the London Poor* (vol. 3).

78 American Kennel Club, "Teddy Roosevelt terrier."

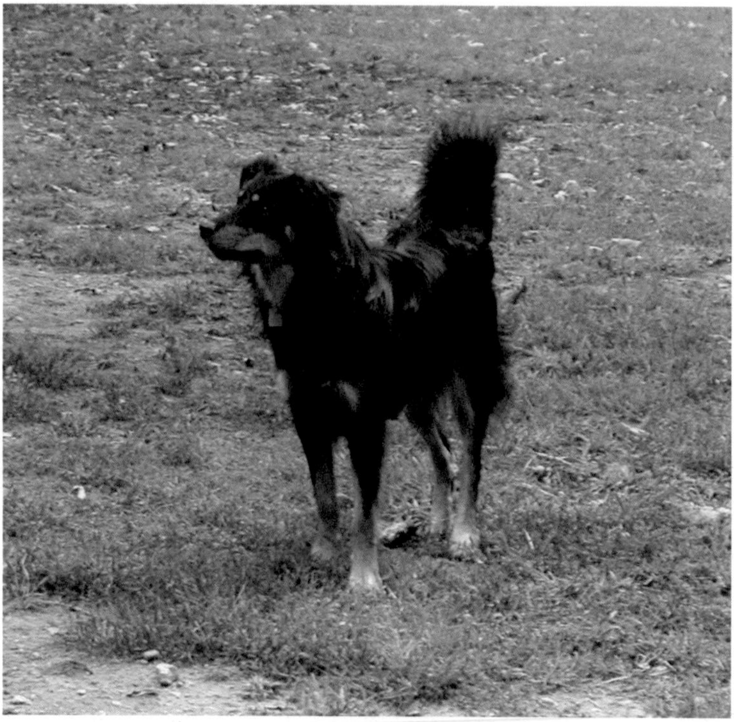

Fig. A1.2 Image courtesy of Rebecca Wingler/ whiteoakenglishshepherds.com.

THE ENGLISH SHEPHERD

There is a breed which will one day be recognized as a registered breed by the foremost kennel associations, [and] which has no commonly recognized name. It is known variously as the farm shepherd, the barnyard collie, the old fashioned shepherd, the cow dog, the English shepherd, and by other colloquial names. And while I doubt there is a more alert, trustworthy, or American dog, still no breed specialty clubs have been organized to push it. The hound and this old fashioned cow dog have gone hand in hand with the early de-

velopment of this country. Nowhere have either had greater usefulness.
Whitney, 1937

The cur and the feist were features of the southern frontier, with their refugia in the South.

These dogs are known by a number of names. I will call them English shepherds because that's what Tom Stodghill called them. The United Kennel Club has been registering English shepherds since the 1920s, but Tom was instrumental in forming the English Shepherd Club of America around 1950. Tom's great-grandparents had been among the settlers who brought the English shepherd's ancestors to the United States. The Animal Research Foundation registered their first English shepherd in 1950, the year before they registered their first Catahoula.[79]

The English shepherd is about as tall as its cousin, the border collie, but can be a little stockier. Many English shepherds are black-and-tan, but they occur in the usual collie colors, except for merle.

The English shepherd is a generalist in an age of specialization. That may cost him some popularity. The English shepherd can handle sheep, but sheep raisers usually use border collies. The English shepherd can control cattle, but Australian cattle dogs and curs are perhaps better at it. The English shepherd can control vermin, but chemical pesticides and barn cats are now used for that. The English shepherd can herd hogs, but curs are better at that. The English shepherd is not as common on American farms as he once was, but, as the English Shepherd Club says, it is still the "American heritage farm dog."[80]

---

79 Tom Stodghill. *Stodghill's Animal Research Magazine.* Spring 1964.
80 "America's Heritage Farm Dog," English Shepherd Club.

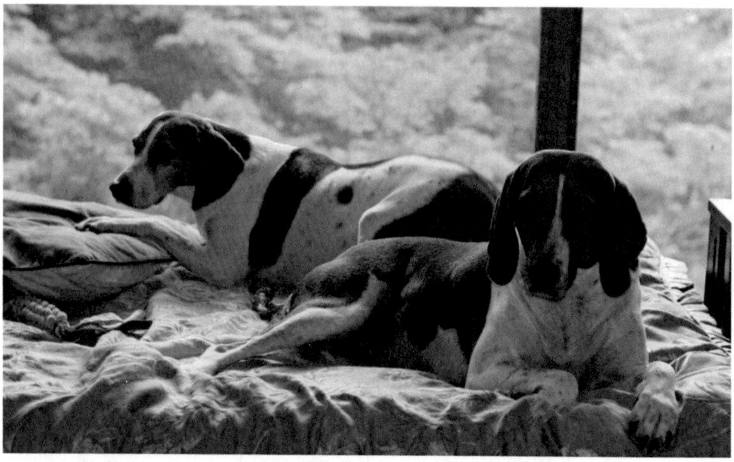

Fig. A1.3 "Eve & Mary." Two tricolor coonhounds.
Image courtesy of Saiberiac, flic.kr/p/VpZR6c.

THE SCENT HOUND

Throughout American history, scent hounds have been more popular than curs, feists, or English shepherds. They were and are used wherever hunters wanted a dog that would follow scent trail. Today, scent hounds of a number of breeds are used all over the U.S. Even in cities some hunters keep a few hounds (typically beagles or coonhounds).

Unlike the ancestors of English shepherds, feists, and curs, which were brought to North America by farmers or other working-class people, scent hounds were brought to America by both working class people and by educated upper class men, some of whom kept packs of hounds as a hobby. Farmers seldom kept written records of their dogs, but fortunately, the landed gentry did.

Robert Brooke came to Maryland when he was appointed governor in 1650. Brooke brought his pack of scent hounds, many of which were black-and-tan. The Brooke family maintained hounds in America at least until 1940.[81]

The only English noble to settle in the colonies was Thomas, Baron Cameron, Sixth Lord Fairfax. Lord Fairfax immigrated to Virginia with his pack of scent hounds in 1748, met the sixteen-year-old George Washington, and later hired him to survey his lands in western Virginia. Washington was already interested in animals, but his developing friendship with Lord Fairfax whetted his interest in scent hounds and fox hunting. Fairfax's dogs probably included English foxhounds.

As an adult, Washington collected and bred scent hounds. During the American Revolution, Washington's friend the Marquis de Lafayette told him about the foxhounds in the French king's kennels. Washington expressed interest in including that breed in his breeding program and, after the war, Lafayette sent seven of these dogs to Washington. They were called Grand Bleu de Gascogne and were colored like modern bluetick coonhounds, white with gray tics.

By 1785, Washington's dogs included descendants of hounds imported by Robert Brooke in 1650, 135 years earlier. Washington was given some hounds by Lord Fairfax. With these, the seven Grand Bleu de Gascogne, and possibly others, Washington led the development of the American foxhound.[82]

The existence of an animal unknown in Europe opened a new niche for scent hounds in North America. That animal was the raccoon, the clever, masked animal whose paws are as dexterous as our hands. Foxhounds are beagles that were used to hunt coon, but are better at hunting animals that don't climb (foxes, rabbits, weasels). Raccoons and some

---

81 J. Blan van Urk.

82 "American Foxhound," akc.org

other animals (possums, bobcats, squirrels) often climb to escape dogs. Coonhounds are treeing dogs, uniquely adapted for that challenge.

Almost any dog will stay at the base of a tree and bark if it knows there's an animal up there. I've known and walked dogs of many breeds, but a German shepherd-coonhound mix my daughter owned was the best squirrel spotter I've ever seen. Her name was Jasmine (we called her Jazz) and I used to walk her, a border collie, and a dachshund at the same time. Often, we'd pass under a tree with a squirrel in its branches. The border collie, the dachshund, and I would have passed oblivious to any squirrel but for Jazz. If Jazz had had wings, that squirrel would have been a goner. One important quality a treeing dog must possess is awareness of animals overhead.

A number of coonhound breeds have been developed over time. Among the most popular are the bluetick, the redbone, the black-and-tan, and the treeing Walker (called the treeing Walker to distinguish it from the Walker foxhound).

People generally become devoted to their dogs, some so much that they will have them buried in a pet cemetery, but some coonhounds are laid to rest with even more honor. In Colbert County, Alabama, there is a cemetery reserved for great coonhounds.[83]

83 CoonDawgs.com

APPENDIX II
INHERITANCE OF MERLING AND THE HARLEQUIN CONDITION

MERLING

The gene for merling (M) is dominant over the gene for "some other coat condition" (m); therefore, a dog with the genotype Mm will be merled. If a dog inherits a gene for merling from each parent, its genotype will be MM; this a double merle. It will be white or almost all white and have defective eyesight and hearing. Breeders try to avoid producing double merles. The genotype of a dog that is not merled will be mm. The dog could be any color, but the genotype will still be mm.[84]

1 parents	**2 M**	**3 m**
4 M	5 MM (double merle)	6 Mm (merle)
7 m	8 Mm (merle)	9 mm (non-merle)

Punnett Square #1: Merle mated with merle: Mm x Mm.

Expected ratio: 1 double merle to 2 merles to 1 non-merle (1:2:1).

Geneticists use a simple device called a Punnett Square to help predict the outcomes of matings. Punnett Square #1 describes the mating of two Catahoula leopards, or two merled dogs of any breed. The genes from one parent (an M and an m) are written across the top of the square, in

84 Paw Print Genetics

cells 2 and 3. The genes from the other parent, in this case also an M and an m, are written vertically on the left side of the Punnett Square, in cells 4 and 7. The interior cells, 5, 6, 8, and 9, contain possible genotypes of puppies born of this mating. One of the four cells (5) contains the genotype MM, so a puppy in this litter has a one in four chance of being a double merle. Another of the four cells (6 and 8) show Mm, so a puppy has a two in four chance of being merled.

Another way to look at this situation is to think of the litter as consisting of ¼ double merles, ¼ non-merled puppies, and ½ merles. This is an approximation but over a large number of Mm X Mm matings, it comes close to the actual outcome. Since mating merle X merle may produce dogs with defective eyesight and hearing (double merles), breeders try to avoid it.

1 parents	**2 M**	**3 m**
4 m	5 Mm (merle)	6 mm (non-merle)
7 m	8 Mm (merle)	9 mm (non-merle)

Punnett Square #2: Merle mated with non-merle: Mm x mm.

Expected ratio: 1 merle to 1 non-merles to (1:1).

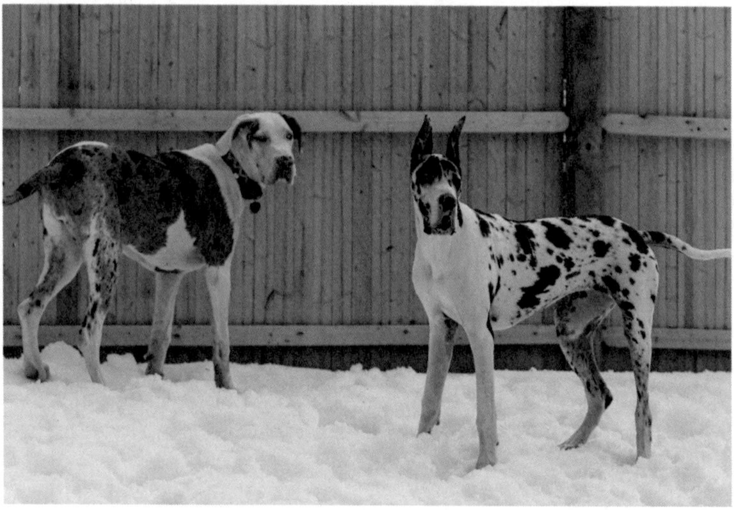

Fig. A2.1 A merled Great Dane (left) and a harlequin Great Dane (right). Image courtesy of Bill Marquardt.

HARLEQUIN

Harlequin Great Danes are merled, and must have Mm as part of their genotype. In addition, they must possess a gene for the harlequin condition. Harlequin Great Danes have a snow-white background and large jet-black patches. The AKC calls these "torn black patches." The harlequin's appearance is different from the usual merle because it possesses a gene which modifies merle. The harlequin gene is found only in Great Danes. The harlequin gene (H) is dominant over the gene for "some other coat condition" (h). A harlequin gamete (sperm or egg cell) must contain a gene for either merling (M) or some other coat condition (m), and either a gene for harlequin (H) or some other coat condition (h). A harlequin Great Dane's genotype is HhMm, heterozygous for both harlequin and merling. The harlequin gene is lethal in a double dose. A dog inheriting a H from each parent will die before birth.

Punnett square # 3 shows the results of a mating between two harlequins. Each parent is HhMn, and produces gametes with either H or h and either M or m. Each parent, therefore, produces gametes with the following four combinations: HM, Hm, hM, and hm. A dog inheriting a capital H from each parent will die before birth, since HH is a lethal condition. A dog inheriting a capital M from each parent will be a double merle, likely with poor hearing and eyesight. Squares labeled black represent puppies who are black or mantle (white on the chest, face and legs), but will carry the gene for harlequin. Mantles are sometimes called Bostons because they're colored like Boston terriers.

1 parents	**2 HM**	**3 Hm**	**4 hM**	**5 hm**
6 HM	7 HHMM (lethal)	8 HHMm (lethal)	9 HhMM (double merle)	10 HhMm (harlequin)
11 Hm	12 HHMm (lethal)	13 HHmm (lethal)	14 HhMm (harlequin)	15 Hhmm (black)
16 hM	17 HhMM (double merle)	18 HhMm (harlequin)	19 hhMM (double merle)	20 hhMm (merle)
21 hm	22 HhMm (harlequin)	23 Hhmm (black)	24 hhMm (merle)	25 hhmm (neither merle nor harlequin)

Punnett Square #3: Harlequin mated with harlequin: HhMm x HhMm.

Expected ratio: 4 harlequin to 3 double merle to 2 merle to 2 black to 1 none of the above.

Punnett Square #4 represents a mating of a harlequin (HhMm) with a mantle carrying the harlequin gene (Hhmm).

1 parents	2 HM	3 Hm	4 hM	5 hm
6 Hm	7 HHMm (lethal)	8 HHmm (lethal)	9 HhMm (harlequin)	10 Hhmm (black)
11 hm	12 HhMm (harlequin)	13 Hhmm (black)	14 hhMm (merle)	15 hhmm (neither)

Punnett Square #4: Harlequin mated with mantle carrying harlequin gene: HhMm x Hhmm.

Expected ratio: 2 harlequin to 1 merle to 2 black to 1 neither.

1 parents	2 HM	3 Hm	4 hM	5 hm
6 hm	7 HhMm (harlequin)	8 Hhmm (black)	9 hhMm (merle)	10 hhmm (neither)

Punnett Square #5: Harlequin mated with non-harlequin non-merle: HhMm x hhmm.

Expected ratio: 1 harlequin to 1 black to 1 merle to 1 neither.

WORKS CITED

PRINT WORKS

Abney, Don. *The Louisiana Catahoula Leopard Dog: A Truly Versatile Working Dog*. Wilsonville, OR: Doral, 1966.

———. *The Complete Louisiana Catahoula Leopard Dog*. Wilsonville, OR: Doral, 2010.

American Kennel Club. *The New Complete Dog Book.* 22nd ed. Companion, 2017.

Bartram, William. *Travels through North and South Carolina, Georgia, East and West Florida, the Cherokee Country, the Extensive Territories of the Muscogulgees or Creek Confederacy, and the Country of the Chactaws*. Philadelphia: James and Johnson, 1791.

Basquette, Lina. *How to Raise and Train a Great Dane*. New York: Sterling, 1961.

Baur, John. *Dogs on the Frontier*. San Antonio, TX: Naylor, 1964.

Blanchard, John. "Hog Dogs of the Catahoula." *Forests and People*, 1961, 6–11.

Bradford, Roark. "Roustabouts and Razorbacks." *The Saturday Evening Post*. August 17, 1929. Reprinted in Brown, W. C.

Brown, W. C. (compiler). *The Catahoula Hog Dog*. Privately printed, 1962. Accessed in Catahoula Parish Library, Harrisonburg, LA.

Burnett, Edmond Cody. "Hog Raising and Hog Driving in the Region of the French Broad River." *Agricultural History* 20, no. 1 (April 1946): 86–103.

Charlevoix, Pierre F. X. de. "Historical Journal of Father Pierre François Xavier de Charlevoix." In French, B. F. Historical Collections of Louisiana. New York: D. Appleton and Company, 2004.

Clark, James C. *200 Quick Looks at Florida History.* Sarasota, FL: Globe Pequot/Pineapple Press, 2000.

Derr, Mark. *A Dog's History of America: How Our Best Friend Explored, Conquered, and Settled a Continen*t. New York: North Point, 2004.

Deuteronomy 23:18 (KJV).

Drake, Richard B. *A History of Appalachia*. Lexington, KY: The University Press of Kentucky, 2001.

Duncan, Davin Ewing. *Hernando De Soto: A Savage Quest in the Americas*. Norman: University of Oklahoma Press, 1997.

The Economist. March 30, 2019.

Faulkner, William. "The Bear." In *Big Woods: The Hunting Stories*. New York: Random House, 1955.

French, Benjamin Franklin, ed. *Historical Collections of Louisiana*. New York: Wiley and Putnam, 1846.

Hardin, Garrett. "The Tragedy of the Commons." *Science* 162, no. 3859 (Dec. 1968): 1243–48.

Hilliard, Sam. *Hog Meat and Hoe Cake: Food Supply in the Old South, 1840–1860*. Carbondale: Southern Illinois University Press, 1972.

———. "Pork in the Antebellum South: The Geography of Self-Sufficiency." *Annals of the Association of American Geographers* 59, no. 3 (Sept. 1969): 461–77.

Hopewell, Clifford. *James Bowie, Texas Fighting Man: A Biography.* Austin, TX: Eakin, 1994.

Kantor, Shawn E. *Politics and Property Rights: The Closing of the Open Range in the Postbellum South*. Chicago: University of Chicago Press, 1998.

Kilpatrick, Alfred R. "Early Life in the Southwest: The Bowies." *De Bow's Review of the Southern and Western States* 13, (1852): 378–83.

King, J. Crawford. "The Closing of the Southern Range: An Exploratory Study." *The Journal of Southern History* 48, no. 1 (Feb. 1982): 53–70.

Kroeber, Alfred. "Cultural Element Distribution XV; Salt, Dogs, and Tobacco." *Berkeley Anthropological Records* 21, no. 1 (1941): 1–20.

Leon-Portilla, Miguel, ed. *The Broken Spears*. Boston: Beacon, 1962.

Le Page du Pratz, Antoine S. *The History of Louisiana or of the Western Parts of Virginia and Carolina*. Paris: De Bure, 1758.

Loughmiller, Campbell, and Lynn Loughmiller. *The Big Thicket Legacy*. Austin: University of Texas Press, 1977.

Louisiana Tourist Development Commission. "The Catahoula Hog Dog Was Hunting Here When Spanish Conquistadores First Stomped into the South." Baton Rouge: Louisiana Tourist Development Commission, 1966.

Meadows, M. E. "Eradication Program in the Southeast United States" *Symposium on the Eradication of the Screwworm from the United States and Mexico.* Misc. Pub. Entomological Society of America 62, (1985): 8–11.

Mims, Sam. "Hog Dogs." *Farm Quarterly.* 5, no. 1 (1950): 77.

Olmstead, Frederick Law. *A Journey through Texas; Or, A Saddle Trip on the Southwestern Frontier.* Austin: University of Texas Press, 2004.

Osler, E. B. "Tonty, Henri." *Dictionary of Canadian Biography Vol. 2.* Toronto: University of Toronto Press, 1969.

Perceval-Maxwell, M. *The Scottish Migration to Ulster in the Reign of James I.* London: Routledge, 1973.

Plott, Bob. *Strike and Stay: The Story of the Plott Hound.* Charleston, SC: History Press, 2007.

Rice, Philip F., and John I. Dahl. *Hunting Dogs*. New York: Harper and Row, 1967.

Sponenberg, D. Philip. "Inheritance of the Harlequin Color in Great Dane Dogs." *Journal of Heredity* 75, (1985): 78.

Stodghill, Tom. "History Registering Catahoula Leopard Cowhogdogs and English Shepherds." *Stodghill's Animal Research Magazine*, Spring 1964.

———. "Stockdog Trials to be Held." *Stodghill's Animal Research Magazine*, Winter 1968.

Taylor, Robert A. "Rebel Beef: Florida Cattle and the Confederate Army, 1862–1864." *The Florida Historical Society Quarterly* 67, no. 1 (July 1988): 15–31.

The American Heritage Dictionary, Fifth Edition. Houghton Mifflin Harcourt Publishing Company. 2020.

Tonti, Henri. "Memoir." In B. F. French, ed. *Historical Collections of Louisiana*. New York: Wiley and Putnam, 1846.

Van Urk, J. Blan. *The Story of American Foxhunting: From Challenge to Full Cry*. New York: Derrydale, 1940.

Wagner, John P. *The Boxer*. New York: Orange Judd, 1952.

Walker, Laurence C. *Forests: A Naturalist's Guide to Woodland Trees*. Austin: University of Texas Press, 1990.

Webb, Jim. *Born Fighting*. New York: Broadway Books, 2004.

Whitney, Leon F. *How to Breed Dogs*. New York: Howell Book House, 1966.

Wigginton, Eliot. *Foxfire 3*. New York: Knopf Doubleday, 1975.

ONLINE SOURCES

American Kennel Club. "Foundation Stock Service." American Kennel Club. n.d. Accessed January 2017. https://www.akc.org/dog-breeds/foundation-stock-service/.

American Kennel Club. "Teddy Roosevelt Terrier". American Teddy Roosevelt Terrier Club. n.d. Accessed December 10, 2008. https://www.akc.org/dog-breeds/teddy-roosevelt-terrier/.

CoonDawgs.com. "Key Underwood Memorial Graveyard." CoonDawgs.com. Accessed December 19, 2008. https://www.coondogcemetery.com/.

Donnelly, Colm J. "Masshouses and Meetinghouses: The Archeology on the Penal Laws in Early Modern Ireland." *International Journal of Historical Archeology* 8, no. 2. (2004): 119–32. http://www.jstor.org/stable/20853048. Accessed 21 Oct. 2020.

Ehlers, Sabine. "How much intelligence is inherited in dogs?" *Quora*. Accessed March 17, 2021. https://quora.com/How-much-intelligence-is-inherited-in-dogs.

Encyclopedia of Alabama. "Natchez Trace/Encyclopedia of Alabama." *The Encyclopedia of Alabama*. February 20, 2009. Accessed August 22, 2019. http://encyclopediaofalabama.org/article/h-2037.

English, Geoffrey. "Field Dogs vs Show Dogs." Gusdogs Online. Accessed May 2017. http://www.gundogsonline.com/Article/field-vs-show-hunting-dogs-Page1.htm.

English Shepherd Club. "America's Heritage Farm Dog." Accessed Feb. 20, 2021. https://www.englishshepherd.org.

Faranda, Tom. "What Jim Bowie's Mother Said, after She Was Told Of His Death at the Alamo." *Tom Faranda's Folly*. Last modified January 3, 2009. Accessed August 11, 2019. https://tomfaranda.typepad.com/folly/2009/01/what-jim-bowies-mother-said-after-she-was-told-of-his-death-at-the-alamo.html.

Frisk, Charles. "Spaniels in the Field & Flushing Retrievers." SITFFER Foundation. Accessed May 2017. https://www.spanielsinthefield.com.

Kelly, Patrick. "The Irish Woolen Export Prohibition Act of 1699: Kearney Revisited." *Irish Economic and Social History* 7 (1980): 22–44. http://www.jstor.org/stable/24337085. Accessed 21 Oct. 2020.

Langevin, Mary. "Cats Cradle Catahoulas." Cats Cradle Catahoulas. Accessed September 2, 2019. http://www.catscradlecatahoulas.com/html/what_is_a__cur__dog_.html.

"L. H. Ladner's Yellow Blackmouth Curs." L. H. Ladner's Yellow Blackmouth Curs. Accessed May 1, 2007. https://www.lhladnerblackmouthcurs.com/.

"Louisiana 2017–2018 Hunting Regulations." Louisiana Department of Wildlife and Fisheries. Accessed September 2, 2018. https://www.fs.usda.gov/Internet/FSE_DOCUMENTS/fseprd557350.pdf.

Louisiana Revised Statutes 3:2891. "Swine Prohibited from Running at Large." State of Louisiana. Accessed September 2, 2018. https://law.justia.com/codes/louisiana/2012/rs/title3/rs3-2891/.

National Lacy Dog Association. "History." Accessed January 4, 2008. http://nationallacydog.org/history.html.

Omniglot. "Pennsylvania German (Pennsilfaanisch Dietsch)." Omniglot.com. Accessed August 8, 2019. https://omniglot.com/writing/pennsylvaniagerman.htm.

Online Dictionary. Accessed February 16, 2021. https://googledictionary.freecollocation.com/meaning?word=feist.

Original Mountain Cur Breeders' Association. "A Background Sketch of the Mountain Cur Dog and the Original Mountain Cur Breeders' Association." Omcba.homestead.com. Accessed May 1, 2007. http://omcba.homestead.com/index.html.

Paw Print Genetics. "H Locus (Harlequin, Great Dane Type)." Accessed April 14, 2021. pawprintgenetics.com/products/tests/details/80/.

Snowball Feist Registry. "Snowball Feist History." Home of the Snowball Feist Registry. Accessed December 10, 2008. http://snowballfeist.homestead.com/index.html.

Tanner, Henry. "Sadat in Austria for Ford Meeting." *The New York Times*. Accessed December 1, 2018. https://www.nytimes.com/1975/06/01/archives/sadat-in-austria-for-ford-meeting-says-he-has-nothing-new-to.html

Vincent, George. "Agriculture." University of Tennessee at Knoxville. Accessed August 1, 2019. https://databases.lib.utk.edu/arrowmont/Steve/Agriculture,%206-19.pdf

Wikipedia. "American Foxhound." Wikipedia.org. Last modified August 21, 2019. Accessed December 10, 2008. https://en.wikipedia.org/wiki/American_Foxhound.

———. "Feral Horse." Wikipedia.org. Last modified August 11, 2019. Accessed July 5, 2018. https://en.wikipedia.org/wiki/Feral_horse.

———. "German Palatines." Wikipedia.org. Last modified August 21, 2019. Accessed June 1, 2019. https://en.wikipedia.org/wiki/German_Palatines.

———. "Germantown, Philadelphia." Wikipedia.org. Last modified July 30, 2019. Accessed July 30, 2019. https://en.wikipedia.org/wiki/Germantown,_Philadelphia.

———. "List of U.S. State Dogs." Wikipedia.org. Last modified September 3, 2019. Accessed January 31, 2018. https://en.wikipedia.org/wiki/List_of_U.S._state_dogs.

———. "Plott Hound." Wikipedia.org. Last modified July 16, 2019. Accessed August 8, 2019. https://en.wikipedia.org/wiki/Plott_Hound#History.

———. "Presbyterianism#lreland." Wikipedia.org. Last modified August 13, 2019. Accessed August 14, 2019. http://en.wikipedia.org/wiki/Presbyterianism#lreland.

———. "Rat-baiting." Wikipedia.org. Last modified August 9, 2019. Accessed December 10, 2008. https://en.wikipedia.org/wiki/Rat-baiting.

———. "RatTerrier." Wikipedia.org. Last modified July 2019. Accessed September 6, 2011. https://en.wikipedia.org/wiki/Rat_Terrier.

———. "Restoration_(England)#Religionsettlement." Wikipedia.org. Last modified August 17, 2019. Accessed August 20, 2019. https://en.wikipedia.org/wiki/The_Restoration.

———. "Scotch-lrish_American#Conflict_with_ Native _Americans." Wikipedia.org. Last modified August 29, 2019. Accessed July 30, 2019. https://en.wikipedia.org/wiki/Scotch-Irish_Americans.

———. "Spike (dog)." Wikipedia.org. Last modified May 3, 2020. Accessed February 5, 2021. https://en.wikipedia.org/wiki/Spike_(dog).

———. "Ulster_Scots_people." Wikipedia.org. Last modified August 21, 2019. Accessed August 17, 2019. https://en.wikipedia.org/wiki/Ulster_Scots_people.

Working Catahoula Association. "History of the WCA." Working Catahoula Association. Accessed May 2017. https://workingcatahoulaassociation.com/history-of-the-wca/.

———. "WCA Louisiana 2016 Results." Working Catahoula Association. Accessed March 15, 2017. https://workingcatahoulaassociation.com/.

ACKNOWLEDGEMENTS

Most books are not the product of just one author, and this one is no exception. Many of the people who helped me are mentioned in the text. Photographs and maps are credited, and names (sometimes changed) of my hunting companions appear where hunting trips are described. I'm grateful to Howard Mielke, who put the photographs into JPEG so that they could be published.

I am also grateful to my proofreaders, Lisa Williams, Linda LeBon and Nicholas Guirovich, and to Laura LeBon for sharing the driving to Natchez and all over Catahoula country. I thank Linda Balfour, a descendent of steam boat captains, for information about the steam boats which plied the rivers and Catahoula Lake in the nineteenth century.

Finally, I owe a lot to the people who tried to make up for my computer deficiencies. These brave souls include my wife, Linda LeBon, my daughters, Laura LeBon, Lisa Williams, and Leslie Dewberry, and my grandsons, Nicholas and Alex Guirovich.